TO
DRAW
CLOSER
TO
GOD

TO
DRAW
CLOSER
TO
GOD

A Collection of Discourses
by
Henry B. Eyring

DESERET BOOK COMPANY, SALT LAKE CITY, UTAH

Library of Congress Cataloging-in-Publication Data

Eyring, Henry B., 1933–
   To draw closer to God : a collection of discourses / by Henry B. Eyring.
     p.   cm.
   Includes bibliographical references and index.
   ISBN 1-57345-267-X
   1. Christian life—Mormon authors. I. Title.
BX8656.E96   1997
248.4'89332—dc21
                                 97-19434
                                    CIP

Printed in the United States of America   18961

10 9 8 7 6 5 4 3 2 1

CONTENTS

PART 1

HEARING

EARS TO HEAR

On April 5, 1985, President Gordon B. Hinckley called me to serve as a counselor to Bishop Robert D. Hales in the Presiding Bishopric. I was grateful for the call and for the knowledge that it is the Savior who makes such calls through his servants in his Church.

After I was sustained the next day in general conference, I was overwhelmed in two ways by the reaction of the General Authorities. First, they expressed love and confidence, which I deeply appreciated. But second, I felt an added expression of almost solicitude. I realized they knew what was ahead of me, and I sensed they might know the growing feeling in my heart that I was overwhelmed by the task ahead. As that feeling increased, I began to think more and more of me. But then I remembered that all of us receive callings that stretch our faith. For instance, in the past few weeks a deacon has come home with the rolls to announce that he is the new quorum secretary; a teacher has been called to preside in his quorum; a mother has been called to be a counselor in a Relief Society presidency; and

---

From a talk given at General Conference, 7 April 1985.

a nineteen-year-old boy has been called to go to a new city with a new missionary companion. To each of them, and to each of you, fear of failure might try to poke its head in, as it had with me.

On the day I was sustained to serve in the Presiding Bishopric, something happened that was of great help to me, and it may be of help to you. At that moment, the fear left. It was when Bishop Hales was speaking in conference. He mentioned that we had known each other since boyhood, and as he did a memory was replayed in my mind. It was of a hotel ballroom in New Brunswick, New Jersey. Bishop Hales was likely not there, since he lived in what seemed to us the well-established stake in New York. We were in the New Jersey district, a single district that covered much of the state. The Princeton Branch met in my parents' dining room. Dad was the branch president. Mother was both the pianist and chorister (which is hard to do if you think about it). There was not another family in the branch with children, so my brother Ted was the Aaronic Priesthood, and my brother Harden and I were all there were of Primary and junior Sunday School. The congregations were young students who happened to be there and a few older converts—none with spouses who were members.

There was no building, no gym, no stake center, and so we traveled to a hotel ballroom for what must have been a district conference. I was sitting on a folding chair somewhere near the back, next to my mother. I must have been very young because I can remember putting my legs through the back of the chair and sitting aft instead of forward. But then I remember hearing something—a man's voice from the pulpit. I turned around and looked. I still remember that the speaker was at a rostrum set on wooden risers. There was a tall window behind him. He was the priesthood visitor. I don't know who he was, but he was tall and bald, and he seemed very old to me.

He must have been talking about the Savior or the Prophet Joseph, or both, because that was all I remember hearing much about in those days. But as he spoke, I knew that what he said came from God and that it was true, and it burned in my heart. That was before scholars told me how hard it was to know. I just knew with certainty—I knew it was true.

You can have that same confidence, not of yourself but from God. He lives, and he communicates with his children. This is the Church of Jesus Christ, and he leads it. No assignment in it need ever overwhelm you if you know that and listen for the Master's voice.

Now, I can hear the young deacons saying, "Well, now, that may be fine for you, but surely you don't think that's going to help me in my assignment down here in this deacons quorum." Oh yes, I do. Between being a high councilor and a member of the general board of the Sunday School, I was a deacons quorum adviser. A boy, the president, presided in the meetings, and I taught the lessons out of the scriptures and out of the manual. I stayed very close to the lessons as they were outlined.

I remember one boy in the quorum had to miss a few meetings, so he sent his brother to the class with a tape recorder. His brother recorded our meeting and took it home. It happened more than once. When the deacon came back, I asked him why. I don't remember his words, but I remember that it was clear he knew what I knew. God was trying to speak to that deacons quorum. The boy wasn't anxious to have a tape recording to hear *me*; he was trying to hear God. He knew where to listen and how to hear.

He'd read the scriptures for us in class, and I knew he knew them and loved them. And so, even when I wasn't teaching very well, by the power of the Holy Ghost and from knowing the master's voice in the scriptures, he could hear what he needed to hear. The memory of that black recorder with its tape turning will always remind me of the scripture which says, "He that hath ears to hear, let him hear" (Matthew 11:15).

I spoke at his funeral just a few years later. He lived about as many years as the Prophet Joseph had lived when he saw God the Father and Jesus Christ in the grove. My deacon hadn't seen a vision, but he had heard the voice of God through his servants in a deacons quorum. He wanted to hear, he knew how, and he had the faith he could. Like the boy prophet Joseph, he knew the heavens were open.

If you and I will study the scriptures and pray and tune our hearts and ears, we will hear the voice of God in the voice of the people that he has sent to teach and guide us and direct us. I hear it whenever I attend general conference. You and I can take confidence in that assurance. However large the kingdom will grow—and it will fill the earth—you will not ever feel lost or forgotten, and you need never feel overwhelmed. God will call people to care about you and to teach you. And if you will listen and hear the voice of God, the kingdom will roll forth to its appointed place, ready for the coming of the Master.

None of us can see now all the wonders of technology and organization and buildings that God may give us; but you, just you, hearing the voice of God through your teacher and leader, will always be at its heart.

I'm grateful for the gift given to me of ears to hear. One of my great-grandfathers, John Bennion, walked or rode his horse from over Jordan to general conference to hear his name called out to go on a mission to Dixie. His journal doesn't say much, except just that he prepared to go, and he went. His assignment was to be a sheepherder. In his journal there is a record of an evening in which he met with Erastus Snow. He said another man was in the room; his name was Henry Eyring. And somewhere in St. George that night was Bishop Miles Romney. They talked about sheep. And you might have thought they were talking about something temporal. But not to those men, because they knew the sheep were for God's people. And they knew how to listen, and they knew how to do what they heard.

John Bennion went on another mission to Wales and back again to the Salt Lake Valley. Henry Eyring went on to Colonia Juarez, as Miles Romney did. And they left for me a tradition which I deeply appreciate. They were the yeomen of the Church, the soldiers of the Church, and they were my great-grandfathers. You can't find in their journals records of the positions they held, just of the instructions they heard, and knew were from God, and followed. I'm grateful to my parents who handed me that heritage undiminished. I'm grateful to my wife, who more than once has heard the voice of the Spirit when I did not and has gently said, "Would you pray about it?" If my sons and daughters will listen to her, and hear through her what God has in mind for them, we will pass the heritage on again.

I testify that God loves his children and can tell us what is true. I pray that we all may have ears to hear, that he may guide us.

CHAPTER 2

"LISTEN TOGETHER"

I believe the Savior was speaking to you and me in the very first verse of the Doctrine and Covenants. It reads: "Hearken, O ye people of my church, saith the voice of him who dwells on high, and whose eyes are upon all men; yea, verily I say: Hearken ye people from afar; and ye that are upon the islands of the sea, listen together." (D&C 1:1.)

In the Lord's church, we all have opportunities to learn how to "listen together."

Whenever stake presidencies and bishoprics call new leaders and teachers in stake and ward organizations, it's a time of testing for the members. You may have experienced such a test yourself. You may have been disappointed that you were overlooked, or you may have been glad you were not called. On occasion, you may have wondered about a person who was called whose weaknesses you knew. Perhaps someone was called—someone you were expected to follow—whom you didn't admire or perhaps didn't even like.

I bear you a testimony of two things which I pray the Spirit will confirm to you. First, God directs those who issue

From a talk given at a BYU Fireside, 4 September 1988.

calls to even the apparently minor offices in the Church. And, equally important, God honors and respects those calls to his servants by using them to serve you.

Most of you believe that, and yet you still have a challenge. I have one, too. I have had experiences where even after I had a clear spiritual conviction that a person had been called to lead me or to teach me, it was still hard to really listen to him. You may think that is just your problem. Or you may think, "If only I were in a 'higher' calling, then I wouldn't have to worry about getting my instructions from anyone else." But you know that is not true.

Every Sunday your bishop, for instance, makes a choice whether he will hold some meetings or some interviews or go to a Sunday School class. Teaching that Sunday School class will be someone whose weaknesses he knows and who likely will not have prayed and studied and struggled and served as much as the bishop has in the past week. But the bishop will go. And he, like you, will need to know how to listen.

A few may wonder about the requirement to listen to other people and may ask, "Why do I have to get my direction and teaching from somebody else? Why can't I go to God for myself and get my own revelation? Why can't I have the Holy Ghost inspire me? Why does every call to lead, in fact, call others to listen? Why are we all, therefore, called to listen? Why should even a prophet have a home teacher?"

I don't know all the answers, but this much I do know: the revelations of God make it clear that his voice will sound to all people. We are told that in the first section of the Doctrine and Covenants. It says this: "And the voice of warning shall be unto all people." (D&C 1:4.) That voice, of course, is the voice of God. Verse 2 says, "For verily the voice of the Lord is unto all men." But in verse 4, when it says "the voice of warning shall be unto all people," it concludes with "by the mouths of my disciples, whom I have chosen in these last days."

More than once the Lord simply says you will need to hear his voice, but you will need to hear his voice from him and from his servants. In verse 14 it says: "And the arm of the Lord shall be revealed; and the day cometh that they who will not hear the voice of the Lord, neither the voice of his servants, neither give heed to the words of the prophets and apostles, shall be cut off from among the people."

I know a few of the reasons why the Lord requires us to listen to mortal servants. One of the reasons is that you and I need a check on our own inspiration occasionally. We can be mistaken. At times, even with real intent and with faith and with careful prayer, we may come to wrong conclusions. Listening to others can provide correction. It can promote more careful consideration. I hope you will always remember that there is safety in counsel.

I can think of another reason why we are blessed to be required to be taught by other human beings. For me, that is made clear in the first section of the Doctrine and Covenants, verse 23, which says the Lord intended "that the fulness of my gospel might be proclaimed by the weak and the simple unto the ends of the world, and before kings and rulers."

Now, why in the world would the weak and the simple be sent to kings and rulers? You and I sometimes feel that we are wise and we know a good deal. We have increasing experience. So why should a Sunday School teacher who seems to us weak and simple and less experienced be called by inspiration to teach us?

One reason is that it requires humility on our part. It requires a humble heart to believe that you can be taught

11

by someone who apparently knows a good deal less than you do, and perhaps seems less likely to get revelation.

When I was the president of Ricks College years ago, I remember having a man who was my priesthood leader come to my house each month to interview me about my home teaching. He brought with him a notebook in which he wrote notes. He recorded not only my report as a home teacher, but my observations about the gospel and life as well.

I remember at first being very flattered. Then one Sunday he and I were visiting what was then called junior Sunday School. He was a few rows in front of me. The speaker was a little girl, no more than six or seven, probably not yet old enough to have the gift of the Holy Ghost. I glanced over at the man and noticed with surprise that he had that same notebook open. As the little girl spoke, he was writing with as much speed and intensity as he had in the study of my home. I learned a lesson from him that I haven't forgotten. He had faith that God could speak to him as clearly through a child as through the president of a college.

I watched him over the years. He kept listening, even to children and novices called to teach him. He lived the commandments, he seemed to grow in wisdom, and he served for a time as the bishop. Tragedies of both illness and sin came to his family. Many years have gone by now. I don't know all the facts, but the facts I do know tell me that all his children have come back to productive, happy lives through the blessings of heaven, the power of the Atonement, and the ministrations of that humble father. Those miracles came, I believe in large part, because he could hear the voice of God in words of the weak and the simple.

I doubt that what he wrote in the pages of that binder

over those many years held the secrets he needed to help his children. He may not even have kept the notes. But he practiced listening, and he learned to hear. And so when he was desperate, as you and I will all someday be desperate, he could hear through the Spirit the voice of comfort, direction, and then peace.

If you and I are going to live up to the glorious promises of the first section of the Doctrine and Covenants, I think we will have to learn how to have the everyday faith of my friend with the notebook. You remember verses 20 through 22 of that first section: "But that every man might speak in the name of God the Lord, even the Savior of the world; that faith also might increase in the earth; that mine everlasting covenant might be established."

And you have often heard verse 38 quoted. It is the next to the last verse in the section. It is the way the Lord chooses to end his preface to his Doctrine and Covenants. He says, "What I the Lord have spoken, I have spoken, and I excuse not myself; and though the heavens and the earth pass away, my word shall not pass away, but shall all be fulfilled, whether by mine own voice or by the voice of my servants, it is the same."

Clearly, my problem and your problem is to hear the word of God from and through imperfect teachers and leaders. That is your test and mine. And it is our opportunity. All of us—today, next week, and for the rest of our lives— are going to be sitting somewhere while someone leads us or teaches us who will seem weak and simple because he is human, like us. God has said that if we are going to make it home again, we must not only hear his voice privately by our own effort, but also through the voice of his servants who, when they speak by the power of the Spirit, speak as if it were his voice.

Now the practical question is, How can we do it? Next

Sunday, for instance, you will go into a class where someone will teach you. He will look a little afraid and be imperfectly prepared, no matter how hard he has worked. You will have the challenge not simply to be attentive, but to listen the way my friend with the notebook did. He could hear the voice of God in the words of a child.

Our problem is to have the Spirit confirm to us the truth of the words of our leader or teacher just as it has, for instance, confirmed the words we have read in the Book of Mormon. Most of you, I would hope, have read in the Book of Mormon and have felt something in your heart or in your mind that told you it was true. I bear you my testimony that that is the voice of the Spirit speaking to you. Our pride is less likely to be aroused when we open the book than when a stranger or the fellow who lives down the street begins to speak. Nevertheless, whatever method works when we study alone should work as well when we listen together.

To me, the best directions about how to get the help of the Holy Ghost, directions that I have tested and know to be true, were given by President Marion G. Romney. I will give you his instructions in his own words. Then together let us see if we can figure out how we can work to prepare for that Sunday School teacher or quorum leader or sacrament meeting speaker to whom we will listen next Sunday.

Here are President Romney's instructions: "If you want to obtain and keep the guidance of the Spirit, you can do so by following this simple four-point program. One, *pray*. Pray diligently. Pray with each other. Pray in public in the proper places. . . . Learn to talk to the Lord; call upon his name in great faith and confidence. Second, *study* and learn the gospel. Third, *live righteously*; repent of your sins by confessing them and forsaking them. Then conform to the teachings of the gospel. Fourth, *give service* in the Church."

And then President Romney concludes this way: "If you will do these things, you will get the guidance of the Holy Spirit and you will go through this world successfully, regardless of what the people of the world say or do." ("Guidance of the Holy Spirit," *Ensign*, January 1980, p. 5; emphasis added.)

That four-point program makes no distinction between the moments we seek the Spirit when we are alone in our scripture reading and those moments when we are listening to a human being. I bear testimony that it works in both settings. It takes some extra effort sometimes when the words come from people instead of from the gilt-edged pages of scripture with which you have had long and sacred experience, but it can be done. Let us see how we might make that effort.

Pray Diligently. President Romney began by saying: "Pray. Pray diligently. Pray with each other. Pray in public in the proper places. . . . Learn to talk to the Lord; call upon his name in great faith and confidence."

You might find a moment tonight to get in the proper place, perhaps alone, where you can pour out your heart. Among the things you will pray about, you might ask for a blessing on those who will teach you next Sunday. Try to visualize where you will be and who will teach you.

Next Sunday I will probably find myself sitting in a stake conference. You know how it works; the visiting authority does a lot of listening. I will speak at the end of each meeting I am in, but the rest of the time I will be listening. I will pray for the speakers. I won't know all their names. They may be frightened, and they may be preparing right now. I will pray for them with faith and with confidence. I will talk to God about them and tell him how much I desire for him to teach me through them. And I know that I will be taught things that neither education

15

nor experience nor the previous teaching I have received has ever provided me. From those people I will be taught things of which I will be able to bear testimony.

You may not know who your Sunday School teacher or quorum instructor or Relief Society teacher will be next Sunday, so you may not know their names either, but you can do the same thing. You can pray specifically that the Holy Ghost will come to them as they prepare to teach and again as you sit at their feet to listen.

I'm not sure I understand how this works, but I know it works. A few years ago when I was preparing to speak to a large group of students at Brigham Young University, I felt some impressions of something I was supposed to teach them. These impressions came with more than the normal intellectual force. In fact, I felt the power that I have come to know as the teaching of the Holy Spirit. But something else came. As I received the idea for my talk, I felt with it an impression that I was receiving it because of the prayers of one or more of the young people to whom I would be speaking. Now, I am not so egotistical as to think that many of them even knew I was coming. I wouldn't think I was on very many people's minds, but I must have been on someone's mind. Perhaps it wasn't so much that anyone was naming me, but someone must have been pleading to be given some help, to be taught something, to be given some assurance, and I must have been the most available servant, or at least the one who was going to go there next.

There are limits to that, of course. The companionship of the Holy Ghost is something that you must earn. Your teacher cannot depend upon your faith alone. You cannot with your faith force the attendance of the Holy Ghost on him or her. As you know, when we receive the gift of the Holy Ghost, the Holy Ghost is not told to come to us. We

16

are told to *receive* the Holy Ghost. That is done by our faith and repentance, by our making covenants and accepting ordinances, and then by our working hard to get and keep the gift. Your teacher cannot be compelled by you to receive it, but by your prayers you can and will bring down the blessings of heaven, and particularly the gift of the Holy Ghost, which will help your teachers and your leaders.

Study and Learn. President Romney's second suggestion for obtaining and keeping the guidance of the Spirit was to study and learn the gospel. That won't be hard for you to apply in getting ready for next Sunday either. There will be a lesson in that class next Sunday. With a little effort you could probably get a manual, or with a phone call you could find out what the subject will be. Then you could go to the Topical Guide, or from your own knowledge of the scriptures you could begin to learn something now about what you will listen to then.

Most of you have been teachers at one time or another in the Church, and so you know how rare it is for a student in your class to have done that. You knew who they were. It was not so much what they said, although it may have been in what they asked in the class. It may have been simply the look in their eyes. It may have been their attentiveness. But you knew that some people prior to coming to your class had studied and by doing so had let heaven know that they wanted to be taught. That changed the class, and it changed your teaching.

Live Righteously. President Romney's third injunction was to "live righteously; repent of your sins by confessing them and forsaking them. Then conform to the teachings of the gospel." I hope a day doesn't begin or end that you don't consider whether something you did might have offended the Holy Ghost or made it harder for the Spirit to influence you. That is what it means to me to have a repentant heart.

You might, in addition, be eager to conform to the quiet promptings that urge you to take action. Make a commitment that the next time you are taught by one of the servants of God, you will heed any prompting, even the faintest prompting, to act, to do better. In fact, you could commit to opening your heart to those promptings even while reading these words. That also is the spirit of repentance.

I had that happen to me not long ago. I was sitting in my home ward in the presence of a teacher who said something, and I felt a very faint prompting from the Spirit to act that day. I bear you my testimony that the scriptures are not being poetic when they describe the Holy Ghost as the still, small voice. It is so quiet that if you are noisy inside, you won't hear it. It is real. I felt also that if I didn't do it promptly, I would not again, at least not soon, feel that gentle instruction. So I did it. I am confident that because I went and did the small thing that I felt impressed by the quiet voice to do, I made it more likely that I could receive a spiritual nudge again.

I pray that you will make a commitment to act on those promptings you receive when listening to your teachers and leaders. If you feel a prompting to do something as a result of reading this book, and if you do it, you will reinforce in your life a pattern of repentance—which is to be eager to be instructed, even to be reproved, and then to act.

What the scripture calls a "humble and contrite heart" has always been exemplified for me in two paragraphs from the autobiography of Parley P. Pratt. Perhaps it touched me because I admired so much the strength of Elder Pratt and also because I like so little to be rebuked. Here is the first paragraph of the two (I will have to break between the two to give you a little background):

> After journeying for several hundred miles up the Platte, we at length met two messengers from the pioneers under President Young, from Salt Lake Valley. These were P. Rockwell and E. T. Benson; who had been sent out to try to find us and report our progress and circumstances. Having visited all the camps, they returned to the valley, or rather to where they met the President and pioneers, on their way back to Winter Quarters on the Missouri. I accompanied them back nearly one day's ride on the way, and then bid them God speed, and returned to my own camp. Soon after this our fifty met the President and company of pioneers and camped with them one day.

Now, this is where you need a little background. For a moment, think of yourself as Parley P. Pratt. He was leading a hard, hard march. He was doing the best he knew how. He was an Apostle of the Lord Jesus Christ. He was meeting his leader, one with whom he had passed through great difficulties. Elder Pratt saw himself as an experienced man, as indeed President Young was experienced.

Can you picture yourself having an interview with your priesthood leader? He is going to talk to you about what you have been doing. You have been working hard. Aren't you prepared for a little praise? Wouldn't you like him to tell you how wonderful you are?

Parley P. Pratt had arrived in Winter Quarters after President Young and the Quorum of the Twelve had made some very specific arrangements. Elder Pratt had taken a look at the plans and thought he could do better. He changed the arrangements. He did not know—at least according to one of the other members of the Twelve who had been there—that they were a decision of the Council and were revelation. This is Elder Pratt's description of that day with his priesthood leader:

> A council was called, in which I was highly censured and chastened by President Young and others. This arose in part from some defect in the organization under my superintendence at the Elk Horn, and in part from other misunderstandings on the road. I was charged with neglecting to observe the order of organization entered into under the superintendence of the President before he left the camps at Winter Quarters; and of variously interfering with previous arrangements. In short, I was severely reproved and chastened. I no doubt deserved this chastisement; and I humbled myself, acknowledged my faults and errors, and asked forgiveness. I was frankly forgiven, and, bidding each other farewell, each company passed on their way. This school of experience made me more humble and careful in future, and I think it was the means of making me a wiser and better man ever after. (*Autobiography of Parley P. Pratt* [Salt Lake City: Deseret Book Co., 1985], pp. 330–31.)

Serve in the Church. Fourth, President Romney said to give service in the Church. That works in powerful ways when you are seeking the Holy Spirit and its direction privately. In my life, I have felt the most guidance when I was in God's service, doing something for one of his children.

It can work in the next class or executive meeting you attend in the Church when some very mortal person is in front of you. Rather than thinking, "Well, let's see whether this teacher or leader can convince me" or "How good is he going to be today?" you could think another way. You could say to yourself, "What is it he is trying to accomplish?" Then you could ask yourself quietly, "What can I do to help?"

You will change your whole experience in that hour by making your teacher's or leader's service your service. That choice of an attitude will change the way you listen. Thoughts will come to you during a class or in a meeting that would not come otherwise.

We have mostly considered what can come to you if you apply President Romney's guide as you listen, but there is something even more. Seeking the Spirit can bring you blessings, but seeking to bring it down on someone else also adds the joy of gift giving.

You can give a gift to your teachers and leaders by the way you pray, by the way you study, by the way you have a contrite heart, and by the way you add your service to theirs. You make it more likely that they will feel the power of the Holy Ghost in their service.

Elder Bruce R. McConkie described the magnitude of that gift: "The Holy Ghost is a Revelator; he is a Sanctifier; he reveals truth, and he cleanses human souls. He is the Spirit of Truth, and his baptism is one of fire; he burns dross and evil out of repentant souls as though by fire. The gift of the Holy Ghost is the greatest of all the gifts of God, as pertaining to this life; and those who enjoy that gift here and now, will inherit eternal life hereafter, which is the greatest of all the gifts of God in eternity." (*The Mortal Messiah*, 4 vols. [Salt Lake City: Deseret Book Co., 1979–81], 2:122.)

Now, I have tried to give you some reasons why our Heavenly Father had the Savior organize his church in such a way that we have to be led and taught by his weak and simple servants. And we have talked about how to make it more likely that we can hear the words of God in their words. If we will try to apply President Romney's advice, not just for our own revelation but to bring the Holy Ghost as a revelator to those who lead and teach us, we will add the blessing to our lives of participating in the giving of a gift.

President David O. McKay described what it means

21

when the Holy Ghost comes into a life: "What the sunshine is to the field and to the flowers the Holy Spirit is to the life of man." (*Conference Report*, October 1930, p. 10.) It has been my experience that that sunshine comes into my life even more powerfully when my effort is to try to help those who lead or teach me.

Each time a general conference approaches, you can pray that the Brethren who speak and who lead us will have the Holy Spirit. I will make a twofold promise to you. First, your prayers will be answered if they are offered with faith and with confidence. Second, not only will you bring sunshine to the lives of others, but you will bring sunshine into your own life. As the Brethren speak, you will be able to listen and hear the words of God as he instructs you through his servants. You will recognize the words of truth that you need. And that is sunshine.

President George Q. Cannon gave us a marvelous description of how we can recognize the influence of the Holy Ghost. He said this: "I will tell you a rule by which you may know the Spirit of God from the spirit of evil. The Spirit of God always produces joy and satisfaction of mind. When you have that Spirit you are happy; when you have another spirit you are not happy. The spirit of doubt is the spirit of the evil one; it produces uneasiness and other feelings that interfere with happiness and peace." (*Journal of Discourses*, 26 vols. [London: Latter-day Saints' Book Depot, 1855–86], 15:375.)

I hope you feel happiness. I do. That is an indication that we are on the right course. I can promise you that you can not only feel that now, but you can look forward to it over a lifetime, even a lifetime that may have its trials and its great difficulties.

Years ago I was sitting in a sacrament meeting with my father. He seemed to be enjoying what I thought was a dull talk, given by a member of the stake high council. I watched my father, and to my amazement his face was beaming as the speaker droned on. I kept stealing looks back at him, and sure enough, through the whole thing he had this beatific smile.

Our home was near enough to the ward meetinghouse that we walked home. I remember walking with my father on the shoulder of the road, which at that time wasn't paved. I kicked a stone ahead of me as I plotted what I would do next. I finally got up enough courage to ask him what he thought of the meeting. He said it was wonderful.

Now I really had a problem. My father had a wonderful sense of humor, but you didn't want to push it too far. I was puzzled. I was trying to summon up enough courage to ask him how I could have such a different opinion of that meeting and that speaker.

Like all good fathers, he must have read my mind, because he started to laugh. He said: "Hal, let me tell you something. Since I was a very young man, I have taught myself to do something in a church meeting. When the speaker begins, I listen carefully and ask myself what it is he is trying to say. Then, once I think I know what he is trying to accomplish, I give myself a sermon on that subject." He let that sink in for a moment as we walked along. Then, with that special self-deprecating chuckle of his, he said, "Hal, since then I have never been to a bad meeting."

I don't suppose he used all of the steps I have described to you. He may very well have prayed for that speaker. Over a lifetime he had studied. When he knew what the speaker was trying to say, he had a deep well to go to so he could give himself that sermon.

My father was the kind of man who would have listened to that high council visitor. If he had felt a little pricking in his heart to do something, Dad would have done it. He could listen to anybody. He used to embarrass me when we stopped to get gas because he would seek advice from the gas station attendant. Dad would always treat him as an equal. He would say to me: "Look, I can learn something from anybody. Everyone has had experiences I haven't had."

I think you can have faith and confidence that you will never need to hear an unprofitable sermon or live in a ward where you are not fed spiritually. Wherever you are can always be a place in the kingdom where the first section of the Doctrine and Covenants is not poetry but pure description. These words will be true for you when you are taught in your home or in your apartment or in a class or in a council meeting. These words for you will simply be the truth: "But that every man might speak in the name of God the Lord, even the Savior of the world; that faith also might increase in the earth; that mine everlasting covenant might be established; that the fulness of my gospel might be proclaimed by the weak and the simple unto the ends of the world, and before kings and rulers. . . . What I the Lord have spoken, I have spoken, and I excuse not myself; and though the heavens and the earth pass away, my word shall not pass away, but shall all be fulfilled, whether by mine own voice or by the voice of my servants, it is the same." (D&C 1:20–23, 38.)

I pray with my whole heart that we may listen together and that we may have the gift of the Holy Ghost, both in our private search for truth and as we sit at the feet of the servants of God wherever we may be.

I am blessed in my calling to sit at the feet of prophets. I have spent hours in their presence. I bear you my testimony that the president of the Church is God's prophet upon the earth. I sit with him and hear him speak on a wide variety of issues. He is careful. He speaks with deliberation.

I have had the Spirit confirm to me that the words he spoke were what the Lord would have him speak. I have also sat in a Sunday School class and heard a man who had worked hard to prepare. I have heard him speak words that the Holy Spirit also bore witness to me were true.

The Holy Ghost is real. There is a still, small voice of truth that can speak to you. I pray with my whole heart that you have felt it and that you will feel it in your church meetings. If someone who is trying to serve you calls you on the phone or speaks to you in some way, I hope you will see his human kindness and his interest. But beyond that, I hope you will understand that God's servants are going out across the earth called and empowered by him. They can bring blessings and guidance and help to you. I pray that will come to you, and I pray that you will do all you can to help it come.

LEARNING TO HEAR THE LORD'S VOICE

The love of John Taylor for the Prophet Joseph Smith can easily be felt in the words he wrote about him. The prophet had been martyred. John Taylor was with him at Carthage. Here are his words from what is now the 135th section of the Doctrine and Covenants:

> Joseph Smith, the Prophet and Seer of the Lord, has done more, save Jesus only, for the salvation of men in this world, than any other man that ever lived in it. In the short space of twenty years, he has brought forth the Book of Mormon, which he translated by the gift and power of God, and has been the means of publishing it on two continents; has sent the fulness of the everlasting gospel, which it contained, to the four quarters of the earth; has brought forth the revelations and commandments which compose this book of Doctrine and Covenants, and many other wise documents and instructions for the benefit of the children of men; gathered many thousands of the Latter-day Saints, founded a great city, and left a fame and name that cannot be slain. He lived

---

From a talk given at the Logan Institute of Religion, 19 January 1992.

great, and he died great in the eyes of God and his people; and like most of the Lord's anointed in ancient times, has sealed his mission and his works with his own blood; and so has his brother Hyrum. In life they were not divided, and in death they were not separated! (D&C 135:3.)

You may read that as a loving tribute. But to me it is more than that; it is a statement of fact. "Joseph Smith, the Prophet and Seer of the Lord, has done more, save Jesus only, for the salvation of men in this world, than any other man that ever lived in it." And the sentences that follow suggest why that could be true. Joseph translated the Book of Mormon by the power of God and was the prophet of the restoration which began this last dispensation. That dispensation will extend to every nation, kindred, tongue, and people, and—through the spirit of Elijah and the sealing power—offer the gospel to all who ever lived on the earth. By that giant sweep alone, reaching out to the hosts of God's children living and dead, the Prophet Joseph's contribution to the salvation of the human family is unique among prophets who have served the Savior on this earth.

But there is another way to think about the Prophet Joseph's contribution. Yes, his work will touch the lives of all who have lived on the earth. That is a contribution of breadth. But how has it touched your life? That is another way to think about it: as a contribution of depth. And for you, that will matter more.

There is a danger in deciding who your favorite prophet is, just as there is in having a favorite living General Authority or a favorite bishop of your ward or a favorite visiting teacher. The danger is that you may not listen to the most important messenger to you, who is always the one God sends to you now. Ezra Taft Benson said—before he was the prophet—that the most important prophet to you is the one who is at that moment the Lord's prophet to you. But that is precisely why the Prophet Joseph means so much to me. He has taught me how to listen for God's message, both to me directly and in the words of his servants. Let me tell you how that changes my life every day.

More than for any other prophet, we have a clear and lengthy record from Joseph Smith of how we can communicate with God. Because of Joseph's example and teaching, I can hear what God would have me hear from a living prophet, a bishop of my ward, a home teacher, a child asking a question in my family home evening, or an impression to my heart and mind as I pray.

Your problem and mine is not to get God to speak to us; few of us have reached the point where he has been compelled to turn away from us. Our problem is to hear. The Prophet Joseph is our master example in that art. It helps to think of the process of hearing, which he exemplifies for me, as being in four parts.

First, his words and example teach me *what* to listen for. I can illustrate that best with a true story. I was asked to visit a country in Central America where political conditions had required the Saints to meet in homes rather than in chapels to worship. On the evening of my arrival, I met with the local priesthood leaders. They showed me statistics of attendance, of missionary baptisms, of the retaining of those new members, and of advancements in the priesthood. On every measure they reported to me, the gospel seemed to be entering the hearts of the people better than it had in the past. And yet they had so much less of what we have come to expect and what they had come to expect of facilities and organization.

The happy anticipation I felt in the evening faded some the next morning, a Sunday, as we approached a row of tiny houses down a dirt lane. They were so small, so unlike a church. My heart sank. But as we approached one house, humble enough that you might call it a shack, I looked down and saw that someone had raked the dirt leading from the lane to the front door. The tines of the rake had been swept back and forth carefully to make a perfect, artistic pattern on the hard ground. There was a dog at the front door, shutters but no glass or screens at the windows, and one man in a short-sleeved white shirt standing at the door to greet us.

Inside, ten or eleven people were arranged on boxes and chairs in one of the two rooms. A tiny table stood before the people in the center of the room, with one white cloth on it and another over the emblems of the sacrament. There was no piano or organ, and there were no hymn-books. The two speakers were a girl of ten and a boy of eight. The sacrament was blessed by the only man, who was an elder, and passed by the one Aaronic Priesthood teacher, a young boy. The Sunday School lesson was taught without a manual except for the scriptures. And the two meetings were finished within an hour and a half. No one left when we excused ourselves to go to another meeting at another home. And when they did go, it was to visit the few who belonged to their little congregation who had not come.

I pondered, and you might, too. Why did I hear so clearly in my heart and mind that day the voice of God speaking to me through that little boy and little girl, and from all who spoke—and nearly all spoke—in that Sunday School class? When so much was missing from that place of worship, what allowed that to happen? You would have noticed, as I did, only one striking peculiarity: everyone, as he or she spoke, even those who raised a hand to make a comment in the class—without exception and apparently unable to keep from doing it—bore testimony. They did not speak of the Savior; they said that they knew he had made

30

it possible for their sins to be washed away. They did not speak about Joseph Smith; they said that they knew by the power of the Holy Ghost that he was a prophet. They did not simply discuss chastity or love of neighbor; they said that they knew God blessed them with peace when they kept those commandments.

Because I knew what to listen for in those meetings, I heard it. Joseph Smith taught you and me what to listen for this way: "Salvation cannot come without revelation; it is in vain for anyone to minister without it. No man is a minister of Jesus Christ without being a Prophet. No man can be a minister of Jesus Christ except he has the testimony of Jesus; and this is the spirit of prophecy. Whenever salvation has been administered, it has been by testimony." (*Teachings of the Prophet Joseph Smith*, sel. and arr. Joseph Fielding Smith [Salt Lake City: Deseret Book Co., 1938], p. 160.)

What I listen for is the spirit of testimony, which will be the spirit of prophecy. And I know that salvation will not come to me without my being exposed to that spirit of revelation, of testimony, of prophecy. Because of that, and because I want so much for you to have salvation, I testify that I know that Jesus is the Christ, that he took upon him your sins and mine, that we may become clean and be sanctified if we have faith in Jesus Christ unto repentance and accept the true ordinances of the Gospel; and I testify that the Prophet Joseph Smith saw what he said he saw in the grove, that heavenly messengers restored the power of God to offer those ordinances, and that the keys are held today by Gordon B. Hinckley. God will honor your baptism if you will. God will honor your temple covenants if you will. And if you will, I know as surely as if I had seen it that you will have full salvation, which is eternal life.

If the Holy Spirit will allow it, you will know as you

read these words that Joseph Smith bore true testimony, and it will be as if you can see what he saw:

> And while we meditated upon these things, the Lord touched the eyes of our understandings and they were opened, and the glory of the Lord shone round about. And we beheld the glory of the Son, on the right hand of the Father, and received of his fullness; and saw the holy angels, and them who are sanctified before his throne, worshiping God, and the Lamb, who worship him forever and ever. And now, after the many testimonies which have been given of him, this is the testimony, last of all, which we give of him: That he lives! For we saw him, even on the right hand of God; and we heard the voice bearing record that he is the Only Begotten of the Father—that by him, and through him, and of him, the worlds are and were created, and the inhabitants thereof are begotten sons and daughters unto God. (D&C 76:19–24.)

Now, the second part of listening well—after knowing what to listen for—is *how* to listen. Your natural style of listening, the one that worked best in school, doesn't work as well in hearing what God would have you know. I can remember a professor of physics who looked at my examination paper in advanced theoretical mechanics and asked me with a look of wonder on his face, "You mean you can't see in your mind the curl of a vector?" When I said I couldn't, he shook his head sadly and said, "There must be a place somewhere for you in science, maybe in organic chemistry." I know I may well offend the organic chemists, but to him that would be the last refuge of an intellect unable to grasp the subtleties of vector analysis. I can remember feeling crushed, almost cast out of the sanctuary of science. He rejected me because I was not bright enough, not quick enough intellectually.

But that could not happen to me in God's kingdom. If

you correct me and reveal my weak intellect, I may well be embarrassed, but I will not be discouraged. I will remember the words of the Prophet Joseph, and I will know that my safety is that God is so far my intellectual superior that for him to simplify just a little more for someone like me will be not much more than he must simplify for the brightest human being who lives. To God, we are all infants, and so I take comfort and direction in these words from Joseph Smith: "We may come to Jesus and ask Him; He will know all about it; if He comes to a little child, he will adapt himself to the language and capacity of a little child." (*Teachings of the Prophet Joseph Smith*, p. 162.) And Joseph also taught this later: "The Lord deals with this people as a tender parent with a child, communicating light and intelligence and the knowledge of his ways as they can bear it." (Ibid., p. 305.)

So I can drop the pose and habits of the tough-minded intellectual and know that I may listen as a little child, having confidence that the gospel is simple. In fact, if I listen humbly, with the expectation that what matters most will be clear even to a little child, then I will be both meek enough to be quiet inside—and therefore able to hear the still, small voice—and humble enough to take correction easily. That is how the Prophet Joseph assures me I may listen with confidence: as a little child.

But you might rightly object by saying that the Lord himself taught that much of the gospel is hidden, not easily learned. In fact, there are things called mysteries. Doesn't that sound as if it were complex, available only to the intellectually ambitious? Yes, it sounds that way. But the Prophet Joseph Smith assures me and you that once we receive a simple truth, there is something simple to do to qualify for more truth: we have to live what we learn, with enough humility to obey and enough faith to work at it.

33

That, of course, is a third rule of hearing. You must *listen with the intent of doing what you are told.* If you do, then after you have been obedient you will be told more. Joseph Smith described it this way: "Happiness is the object and design of our existence; and will be the end thereof, if we pursue the path that leads to it; and this path is virtue, uprightness, faithfulness, holiness, and keeping all the commandments of God. But we cannot keep all the commandments without first knowing them, and we cannot expect to know all, or more than we now know unless we comply with or keep those we have already received." (Ibid., pp. 255–56.)

Joseph Smith emphasized the importance of listening with the intent of being obedient by describing what new information will come from obedience. God could reward you with knowing the wonders of his creations, or details about the future, or solutions to complicated problems which have puzzled you. But instead, look at this promise from God through Joseph Smith:

> We would say to the brethren, seek to know God in your closets, call upon him in the fields. Follow the directions of the Book of Mormon, and pray over, and for your families, your cattle, your flocks, your herds, your corn, and all things that you possess; ask the blessing of God upon all your labors, and everything that you engage in. Be virtuous and pure; be men of integrity and truth; keep the commandments of God; and then you will be able more perfectly to understand the difference between right and wrong—between the things of God and the things of men; and your path will be like that of the just, which shineth brighter and brighter unto the perfect day. (Ibid., p. 247.)

If doing right will bring you more knowledge from God, then of all the added knowledge of worth, one of the most precious would be to know better the difference between

34

right and wrong. I don't know what newspaper articles you read most recently or what news reports you saw and heard. But you certainly have had this thought recently: How will I and those I love ever find our way through the increasing flood of filth and sin coming at us? I take courage from Joseph Smith's example and precept; listen for the voice of testimony, listen like a humble child, listen with the intent to obey, then obey, and then have confidence that your capacity to find the safe path—the ability to see and to choose the right—will grow at least in proportion to the confusion ahead.

That suggests the fourth rule of listening: *keep listening,* because you will never know enough in this life. Part of enduring to the end is to never get over being teachable, even after you have lived and learned a lot. The Prophet Joseph gives this counsel to guide you against the day when you become content: "When you climb up a ladder, you must begin at the bottom, and ascend step by step, until you arrive at the top; and so it is with the principles of the Gospel—you must begin with the first, and go on until you learn all the principles of exaltation. But it will be a great while after you have passed through the veil before you will have learned them. It is not all to be comprehended in this world; it will be a great work to learn our salvation and exaltation even beyond the grave." (Ibid., p. 348.)

I've said that Joseph Smith taught me to listen to the Lord's voice by his example. And I suppose that a single morning in his life, the one we all know the best, has in it examples of all we have discussed in this chapter: what to listen for, how to listen, what to do to hear more, and how persistent we should be in our willingness to be taught.

When Joseph Smith, as a boy, went to the grove, he went because he wanted to know the truth. He went to God to know with certainty, not from his reason, what church he should join. To seek the truth from God is to seek testimony; it is to seek revelation. He was not only a child in years, but he was a child in his attitude when he went from his home to the grove on that beautiful morning. He said of himself:

> During this time of great excitement my mind was called up to serious reflection and great uneasiness; but though my feelings were deep and often poignant, still I kept myself aloof from all these parties, though I attended their several meetings as often as occasion would permit. In process of time my mind became somewhat partial to the Methodist sect, and I felt some desire to be united with them; but so great were the confusion and strife among the different denominations, that it was impossible for a person young as I was, and so unacquainted with men and things, to come to any certain conclusion who was right and who was wrong. (Joseph Smith—History 1:8.)

After serious reflection and careful examination of the facts he could gather, and even after his judgment led him in one direction, he felt like a child before a question of such importance. And you remember that when his desire to have true testimony and his attitude of childlike seeking in faith brought the vision, he asked of God the Father and his Son Jesus Christ not just what was true but what he should do. The Savior told him, and he did it. And because he did, the heavens remained opened to him throughout his life. After that first vision, he knew more of what mattered than any person alive, yet he went on listening and learning. And we may be certain that he went on learning, as he prophesied we all will, after he passed into the spirit world, a prophet who sealed his testimony with his blood.

You and I can't hope to describe adequately the contribution of the Prophet Joseph to the cause of the salvation of God's children. But you can gauge what he has done in your life. A few years ago I went with my two young daughters to the Museum of Church History and Art. They wanted to go through the exhibit on Church history. They took with them the little pink sheets printed with questions that the lovely woman at the front desk gave them. While they were writing down the answers to a question about a stone from the Nauvoo temple, I waited for them at the next exhibit. My eyes went to two faces in a glass case, the death masks of Joseph and Hyrum.

It took the girls a long time to write. And it took me a long time to look away from those two faces. And when I did, I walked back again. All the artifacts, all the pictorial accounts of adventures, and even the tragedy portrayed before me melted away, and I could think only of a boy and then a man to whom the heavens were opened, who spoke with God the Father and his Son, who was taught by the angel Moroni, ordained by John the Baptist and by Peter, James, and John, empowered and taught by Moses, Elijah, and heavenly beings beyond his recounting and my comprehension. And most wonderful of all, as I stood there, I could hear the whispering of the Spirit say to me, "It is true."

A handsome couple stopped for a moment beside me. They looked at the exhibits, the woman standing a little to the side, the man with his hands behind his back. They spoke in a European language and then moved quickly off. I could not speak their language. If I had been able to catch them, they might not have understood me. But I know that they, and you, and I, and all of God's children could hear the truth and be led toward salvation if only we knew how to listen and then did it.

I pray that you will try it. You could do it if your home teachers came by to visit. Or you could do it in a conversation with a friend. Or you could pick up the scriptures and start to read—especially in the Book of Mormon, because a modern prophet said so. When President Benson told us to read the Book of Mormon, did you hear more than a man's voice? And did you hear like a child, willing to accept so simple a thing? And did you do it? If you did, and if you will, I will make you a sure promise.

You will learn something that seems new, you will know that it is true, you will find that it is simple, and you will find that it impels you to *do* something. And if you do what you are told, in faith, the cycle of learning will start again, a rung up on that ladder we will climb happily as long as life lasts and beyond.

It would be unfair to end without a warning. This is not simply an invitation to try something pleasant; this is an invitation which involves great blessings when accepted and terrible consequences when rejected. When you listen for the words of God and follow them, you will hear more. When you do not listen or do not follow, you will hear less and less until finally you may not hear at all.

The keys of the Melchizedek Priesthood were restored to the Prophet Joseph Smith. Those keys are held today by the living prophet. They were held by Moses in his day. And the tragedy of Moses' life teaches us that we, by the way we accept or reject God's offer to commune with us, determine not only our own salvation but the opportunities for those who come after us. Listen to this account, which came in revelation to the Prophet Joseph:

> And this greater priesthood administereth the gospel and holdeth the key of the mysteries of the kingdom, even the key of the knowledge of God. Therefore, in the ordinances thereof, the power of godliness is manifest. And without the ordinances thereof, the authority of the priesthood, the power of godliness is not manifest unto men in the flesh; for without this no man can see the face of God, even the

Father, and live. Now this Moses plainly taught to the children of Israel in the wilderness, and sought diligently to sanctify his people that they might behold the face of God; but they hardened their hearts and could not endure his presence; therefore, the Lord in his wrath, for his anger was kindled against them, swore that they should not enter into his rest while in the wilderness, which rest is the fullness of his glory. Therefore, he took Moses out of their midst, and the Holy Priesthood also; and the lesser priesthood continued, which priesthood holdeth the key of the ministering of angels and the preparatory gospel. (D&C 84:19–26.)

I pray with all my heart that you will sense the tragedy in that. I have deep appreciation for the blessings of the Aaronic Priesthood, for the ministering of angels, and for the gospel of repentance. But can you imagine the grief of Moses, of Aaron, and of the people who rejected God's offer to commune with him when they understood what they had lost? We will not lose that blessing again as a people, but you and I could lose it as individuals, and perhaps for all in our families who will come after us.

So I don't just invite you to read the scriptures, to pray, to listen for the word of God. I plead with you. Put yourself where you can hear the words of testimony. Listen with the simplicity of a child. Expect that spirit of testimony and revelation to impel you to action, to keep the commandments. And never think you have been taught enough, that you have listened long enough, that now is your time and turn to rest.

We began with an account of the martyrdom of Joseph Smith. We could well end that way. Let's use the words of an Apostle, Elder David B. Haight: "The last night of Joseph's life on earth, he bore a powerful testimony to the guards and others who assembled at the door of the jail of the divinity of the Book of Mormon, also declaring that the gospel had been restored and the kingdom of God established on the earth. It was for this reason that he was incarcerated in prison, and not because he had violated any law of God or man."

And then Elder Haight recounted the whispered conversation with Dan Jones and the prophecy that he would yet serve a mission in Wales, the coming of the fateful morning, and the afternoon request to John Taylor to sing the song, "The Poor Wayfaring Man of Grief." He sang it twice, reluctantly the second time. Near the end, you remember, are the words:

> *My friendship's utmost zeal to try,*
> *He asked if I for him would die;*
> *The flesh was weak, my blood ran chill;*
> *But the free spirit cried, 'I will!'*

Then Elder Haight said, "And Joseph murmured as an echo to the song, 'I will!'" (Joseph Smith Memorial Sermon, Logan Institute of Religion, 30 January 1983, pp. 7–8.)

You and I may not be asked to face a mob or the bullets of assassins, but we are asked to give our hearts and lives for the Savior. There are simple things to listen for and then to do. I pray that, like Joseph, we will.

PART 2

HEEDING

CHAPTER 4

COME UNTO CHRIST

You have moments when you want to be better than you have ever been. Those feelings may be triggered by seeing a person or a family living in a way that lifts your heart with a yearning to live that way, too. The longing to be better may come from reading the words of a book or even from hearing a few bars of music. For me, it has come in all those ways, and more.

One of my early memories is reading the scriptures in a schoolroom. The law of the land did not yet forbid it, so the Princeton, New Jersey, public schools began each school day with a standard ritual. I can't remember the sequence, but I remember the content. In our classroom, we pledged allegiance to the flag—in unison, standing hand over heart. One student, a different one each school day, read verses he or she had chosen from the Bible, and then we recited aloud together the Lord's Prayer.

So about every twenty-five school days, my turn came to choose the scripture. I always chose the same one, so my classmates must have known what was coming when it was

---

From a talk given at a BYU Fireside, 29 October 1989.

my day. I don't remember when I first heard the words; that is lost in the mists of childhood. But I can recite them to you now, and with them the feelings come back. It happened every time, and it still does: "Though I speak with the tongues of men and of angels, and have not charity, I am become as sounding brass, or a tinkling cymbal. And though I have the gift of prophecy, and understand all mysteries, and all knowledge; and though I have all faith, so that I could remove mountains, and have not charity, I am nothing." (1 Corinthians 13:1–2.)

You remember the rest, through that thirteenth chapter of 1 Corinthians. By the time I read the first few words, the feeling would come back. The feeling was not just that the words were true, but that they were about some better world I wanted with all my heart to live in. For me, the feeling was even more specific, and I knew it did not come from within me. It was that there would or could be some better life, and that it would be in a family I would someday have. In that then-distant future, I would be able to live with people in some better, kinder way, beyond even the best and the kindest world I had known as a boy.

Now, little boys don't talk about such things, not to anyone. You might confide in someone that you wanted to play big-league baseball someday. But you wouldn't say that you knew someday you'd have a home where you would feel the way you felt when you heard the thirteenth chapter of 1 Corinthians. So I never talked with anyone about those feelings.

When I was eleven, my parents dropped me off at the Salt Lake City home of my great uncle Gaskell Romney. He was a patriarch and, because he was my father's uncle, he could give me, a boy from the mission field, a patriarchal blessing. I don't think he even sat down to visit with me. He didn't know me except as my father's son. He just led

44

me through the house to a room where a recording device was on a table. He sat me down facing a fireplace, put his hands on my head, and began to give first my lineage and then a blessing.

He began to tell me about the home in which I would someday be the father. That's when I opened my eyes. I know the stones in the fireplace were there because I began to stare at them. I wondered, "How can this man know what is only in my heart?" He described in concrete detail what had been only a yearning; but I could recognize it. It was the desire of my heart, that future home and family that I thought was secret. But it was not secret, because God knew.

Now, your impressions will not have been quite like mine, but you have felt a tug, maybe many tugs, to be someone better. And what sets those yearnings apart from all your daydreams is that they were not about being richer, or smarter, or more attractive, but about being better. I am sure you have had such moments, not just from my experience, but because of what President David O. McKay once said: "Man is a spiritual being, a soul, and at some period of his life everyone is possessed with an irresistible desire to know his relationship to the Infinite. . . . There is something within him which urges him to rise above himself, to control his environment, to master the body and all things physical and live in a higher and more beautiful world." (David O. McKay, *True to the Faith*, comp. Llewelyn R. McKay [Salt Lake City: Bookcraft, 1966], p. 244.)

That pull upward is far beyond what you would call a desire for self-improvement. When I felt it, I knew I was being urged to live so far above myself that I could never do it on my own. President McKay had it right. You feel an urging to rise above your natural self. What you have felt is an urging from your Heavenly Father to accept this invita-

45

tion: "Yea, come unto Christ, and be perfected in him, and deny yourselves of all ungodliness; and if ye shall deny yourselves of all ungodliness, and love God with all your might, mind and strength, then is his grace sufficient for you, that by his grace ye may be perfect in Christ; and if by the grace of God ye are perfect in Christ, ye can in nowise deny the power of God. And again, if ye by the grace of God are perfect in Christ, and deny not his power, then are ye sanctified in Christ by the grace of God, through the shedding of the blood of Christ, which is in the covenant of the Father unto the remission of your sins, that ye become holy, without spot." (Moroni 10:32–33.)

That urge to rise above yourself is a recognition of your need for the Atonement to work in your life, and your need to be sure that it is working. After all you can do, after all your effort, you need confidence that the Atonement is working for you and on you.

You may feel that upward pull now. I did one afternoon when I came to understand, as I hadn't before, how much I need the Atonement, what I could do to make it work in my life, and what evidence I could have that it was working.

It happened during a devotional at Ricks College. I wasn't the speaker; I was sitting there, just behind and to the right of the speaker. I've still got the set of scriptures that I held that day. It still has the words in the margins that I wrote then, although the page and the book show signs of use.

In my memory, the room that afternoon was almost as light as the sunshine, and just as warm. The speaker was Elder A. Theodore Tuttle of the Seventy. I suppose there was a spotlight on his face. Stages always seem light when you're on them. But the brightness was in more than what I saw. It was inside me that day. I think it happened because

I walked into that room with the yearning President McKay says will come to everyone. And for me that day it was irresistible; I was in the right place with the right preparation.

I had been trying hard, and yet I wanted to know, "Isn't there something more I can do?" And Elder Tuttle told me there was and that I would need the atonement of Jesus Christ working in my life to go where I wanted to go. And so that afternoon lives on the pages of my scriptures, and in my life.

Elder Tuttle began by talking about how someone had passed this understanding on to him. He said he had taken a trip to South America on assignment with Elder Joseph Fielding Smith, then a member of the Council of the Twelve. That was in the days when you went to South America by ship. Elder Smith could have used the time to rest, and he could have let Elder Tuttle rest. But he didn't. He organized daily scripture study, sitting on the deck in those wooden slat chairs most of you have seen only in old movies. They read their scriptures together, and they discussed them, and they marked them. And so what I wrote in my scriptures, in the margins, was written by Elder Tuttle in his Doctrine and Covenants on the ship's deck as Elder Smith taught it to him. I can only imagine who passed it to Elder Smith. And now I'm passing it on to you.

The page on which I wrote is the second page in section 19 of the Doctrine and Covenants, in the old edition of the triple combination. On the bottom of the page, in capital letters, is written the word REPENTANCE. And then an arrow leads to a notation that reads: "Greek word. To have a new mind."

In the very back of my book I had already written a list of words, gospel concepts, and for each one a key scripture. Doctrine and Covenants section 19 became the place where I would ever after turn to find the network of scriptures on repentance that I got from Elder Tuttle's days of being tutored on the deck, sailing south. That was before the invention of the Topical Guide, which I suppose is why I don't build those networks anymore. But he did it for me, and so around the margins of that second page of section 19, I wrote ten scriptural references I got that afternoon with his brief description of why they matter. Somehow he got them all taught, and into my heart, in less than an hour. He was a master teacher. I won't give you all of those scriptures. But I will give you the few that have made the most difference—all the difference for me—in knowing how to reach for that something better you and I sometimes feel drawing us up.

The first is not in the margin but is from the section itself. I heard it that day with new meaning. It begins with the fifteenth verse: "Therefore I command you to repent—repent, lest I smite you by the rod of my mouth, and by my wrath, and by my anger, and your sufferings be sore—how sore you know not, how exquisite you know not, yea, how hard to bear you know not. For behold, I, God, have suffered these things for all, that they might not suffer if they would repent; but if they would not repent they must suffer even as I." (D&C 19:15–17.)

As he read those words that day, I felt the overwhelming suffering of the Savior. And then two things dawned on me. First, if I could not repent to qualify for his atonement for my sins, I must suffer to the limit of my power to suffer. And, second, with all the requisite suffering of my own, with all I could bear, it would still not be enough. I would still be forever shut out of the only place where there will be the warmth of family, the family of my Heavenly Father whom I have loved and whom I miss, and that of my family here. Somehow I had gotten the idea that the choice was between repenting or not. And then I realized that whatever pain repentance might bring in this life, it was certainly no more than the pain I would face if I did not repent here, and yet that later pain could not lift me home. It could not bring the mercy I needed.

A determination flowed into me, both to stay as far as I could from sin and to gain a confidence that my sins were being remitted. In that moment, the penalty for taking chances with sin or with forgiveness loomed larger than I had ever imagined it could. I wanted with all my heart to know both that the Atonement was curing the effects of sin in me and that I was being strengthened against future sin. I wanted to know what I could do to gain assurance that I was on the path home.

Specific steps to assure that the Atonement is at work in your life will not always be the same. For some, at one point, it would be to see a bishop, a judge in Israel, to confess serious sin and to seek help. For another, it would be to accept baptism. But for everyone, at every stage of purification, there are constants. One is this: reception of the Holy Ghost is the cleansing agent as the Atonement purifies you.

President Marion G. Romney taught: "Receiving the Holy Ghost is the therapy which effects forgiveness and heals the sin-sick soul." ("The Holy Ghost," *Ensign*, May 1974, p. 92.) And the Savior said, "Now this is the commandment: Repent, all ye ends of the earth, and come unto me and be baptized in my name, that ye may be sanctified by the reception of the Holy Ghost, that ye may stand spotless before me at the last day." (3 Nephi 27:20.) Moroni also spoke of being wrought upon and cleansed by the power of the Holy Ghost after baptism.

That is a fact you can act on with confidence. You can invite the Holy Ghost's companionship into your life. And you can know when he is there, and when he withdraws.

49

And when he is your companion, you can have confidence that the Atonement is working in your life.

Now, you can make some choices today that will bring the Holy Ghost to you as your companion.

You are called of God to serve his children. You may be called as a clerk or a home teacher or a visiting teacher. You are a son or daughter or a brother or sister. None of those are accidental calls. And each places you in service to invite someone to choose the right, to come unto Christ. None of the people for whom you are responsible can be truly served without your bearing testimony, in some way, of the mission of Jesus Christ.

You know that the mission of the Holy Ghost is to bear testimony of the Savior. When in faith and under assignment you go forth to do that, the Holy Ghost is your ally. The Savior said, "When the Comforter is come, whom I will send unto you from the Father, even the Spirit of truth, which proceedeth from the Father, he shall testify of me." (John 15:26.)

You could, this moment, begin to think of those for whom you bear responsibility. If you do, and do it with the intent to serve them, a face or a name will come to you. If you do something today and make some attempt to help that person come unto Christ, I cannot promise you a miracle, but I can promise you this: you will feel the influence of the Holy Ghost helping you, and you will feel approval. You will know that, for at least those minutes, the power of the Holy Ghost was with you. And you will know that some healing came into your soul, for the Spirit will not dwell in an unclean tabernacle. His influence cleanses.

Not only is your feeling the influence of the Holy Ghost a sign that the Atonement, the cure for sin, is working in your life, but you will also know that a preventative against sin is working.

The effects of the Atonement—the lack of pride, of envy, of malice—are a shield against temptation. The Savior taught that in another of those references written in the margin around my copy of section 19 of the Doctrine and Covenants. It directs me to the first verse in section 95 of the Doctrine and Covenants: "Verily, thus saith the Lord unto you whom I love, and whom I love I also chasten that their sins may be forgiven, for with the chastisement I prepare a way for their deliverance in all things out of temptation, and I have loved you." (D&C 95:1.)

I bear you my testimony that God loves you and that he has prepared a way for your deliverance in all things out of temptation. In that verse the Lord was announcing a chastisement because his people had not built his house as he had commanded. He called that a grievous sin. But the Lord taught that the chastisement that would prepare them to be forgiven would also produce a shield against temptation.

The broken heart and contrite spirit that are the requirements for forgiveness are also its fruits. The very humility that is the sign of having been forgiven is protection against future sin. And it is by avoiding future sin that we retain a remission of the sins of the past.

You may not know when you have been fully baptized with fire and with the Holy Ghost, but you can know you are inviting his presence. And you know when you are making his presence impossible. As you read this book you may be determined to serve the Savior, and thus invite the Spirit, or you might be tempted by some thought like this: "Look, as long as you don't commit great sin, repentance isn't that hard. You just confess, take a little embarrassment, and you are clean again." That is a lie in at least two ways.

First, I have never forgotten the voice of Elder Tuttle as he read this description of suffering for sin from section 19 of the Doctrine and Covenants: "Which suffering caused myself, even God, the greatest of all, to tremble because of pain, and to bleed at every pore, and to suffer both body and spirit—and would that I might not drink the bitter cup, and shrink." (D&C 19:18.)

It was about there that I wrote these words: "Teach the people repentance hurts." You must never believe the lie that there is no pain from sin. You can be forgiven; the Atonement is real. But President Kimball taught that "if a person hasn't suffered, he hasn't repented." (*The Teachings of Spencer W. Kimball,* ed. Edward L. Kimball [Salt Lake City: Bookcraft, 1982], p. 99.) So true faith in the atonement of Jesus Christ, rather than leading you to try a little sin, will lead you to stay as far away from it as you can.

That brings me to a second falsehood. It is this: as the world grows more wicked, it is only reasonable to expect to be overcome by temptation. That is not true either. We do not face so bleak a prospect. President George Albert Smith taught (he said it more than sixty years ago, but it is still true in our time and will be in the future, however dark the world becomes):

> There are two influences ever present in the world. One is constructive and elevating and comes from our Heavenly Father; the other is destructive and debasing and comes from Lucifer. We have our agency and make our own choice in life subject to these unseen powers. There is a division line well defined that separates the Lord's territory from Lucifer's. If we live on the Lord's side of the line Lucifer cannot come there to influence us, but if we cross the line into his territory we are in his power. By keeping the commandments of the Lord we are safe on His side of the line, but if we disobey His teachings we voluntarily cross into the zone of temptation and invite the destruction that is ever present there. Knowing this, how anxious we should always be to live on the Lord's

side of the line. ("Our M.I.A.," *Improvement Era*, May 1935, p. 278.)

The increasing wickedness in the world should not make you *more* inclined to take chances but *less*. By your choice of what you will do and what you won't do, you can place yourself in that territory where the Holy Ghost can be your companion.

Now, you may feel that I have given you only modest hope. You want to know, to be sure—if possible, by some clear sign—that your sins are remitted. So do I. But you and I know that President Ezra Taft Benson was telling the truth when he said: "For every Paul, for every Enos, and for every King Lamoni, there are hundreds and thousands of people who find the process of repentance much more subtle, much more imperceptible. Day by day they move closer to the Lord, little realizing they are building a godlike life. They live quiet lives of goodness, service, and commitment. They are like the Lamanites, who the Lord said 'were baptized with fire and with the Holy Ghost, and they knew it not' (3 Nephi 9:20)." ("A Mighty Change of Heart," *Ensign*, October 1989, p. 5.)

As if he knew my concern, and yours, to discern whether we were moving toward Christ, Elder Tuttle took me to another scripture. Like the others, this reference is written in the margin of section 19 in my old copy of the Doctrine and Covenants. Here is all it says: "Alma 5:14, 15, 26–31." And then these words, written very small: "Born again and retaining remission. How do you know?"

"How do you know?" That was whispered to me after a stake conference by a woman who had tears running down her cheeks. She said: "I've tried so long. I've done everything I know how. Why don't I feel the peace of forgiveness? I want to feel forgiven. I want to feel clean again. I want to feel I can stay that way. How do I know?" It was asked in a letter that came to my desk recently. It was asked the other night on the phone in what began as a call about business. And with tears a young man asked, "Well, how will I know? How do you know?"

Alma the high priest raised that very question, and he answered it as he taught the people in Zarahemla: "And now behold, I ask of you, my brethren of the church, have ye spiritually been born of God? Have ye received his image in your countenances? Have ye experienced this mighty change in your hearts? Do ye exercise faith in the redemption of him who created you? Do you look forward with an eye of faith, and view this mortal body raised in immortality, and this corruption raised in incorruption, to stand before God to be judged according to the deeds which have been done in the mortal body?" (Alma 5:14–15.)

As Elder Tuttle read those words that day, I knew what I wanted. I wanted the Master's image in my countenance, perhaps not visible to others, but so that I might look forward with the eye of faith to that grand reunion. I wanted to have confidence that I would someday and somewhere hear the words: "Come unto me ye blessed, for behold, your works have been the works of righteousness upon the face of the earth." (Alma 5:16.)

As Elder Tuttle moved over a page to read another verse, I wanted to hear how I would know that the Atonement was working in my life. I wanted to know how to retain a remission of my sins. Here is what he read:

> And now behold, I say unto you, my brethren, if ye have experienced a change of heart, and if ye have felt to sing the song of redeeming love, I would ask, can ye feel so now?
>
> Have ye walked, keeping yourselves blameless before God? Could ye say, if ye were called to die at this time, within yourselves, that ye have been sufficiently humble? That your gar-

ments have been cleansed and made white through the blood of Christ, who will come to redeem his people from their sins?

Behold, are ye stripped of pride? I say unto you, if ye are not ye are not prepared to meet God. Behold ye must prepare quickly; for the kingdom of heaven is soon at hand, and such an one hath not eternal life.

Behold, I say, is there one among you who is not stripped of envy? I say unto you that such an one is not prepared; and I would that he should prepare quickly, for the hour is close at hand, and he knoweth not when the time shall come; for such an one is not found guiltless.

And again I say unto you, is there one among you that doth make a mock of his brother, or that heapeth upon him persecutions?

Wo unto such an one, for he is not prepared, and the time is at hand that he must repent or he cannot be saved! (Alma 5:26–31.)

Think of those words: humble, stripped of pride, stripped of envy, not making a mock of my brother, garments cleansed. Have you experienced the change of heart?

I learned a long time ago that it is hard to know how you are doing in being born again, and why it is not easy. Once, as a bishop of a ward, I worked with a young man who had made great mistakes, but he had been moved by faith in the Lord Jesus Christ to make long and painful repentance. We were down to the weeks before he was to be married in the temple. I had long before forgiven him in the name of the Church and had given him his temple recommend. But he remembered that I had said, "The Lord will forgive you in his own time and in his own way," and now he was deeply concerned. He came to my office and said: "You told me that the Lord would someday let me know that I was forgiven. But I am going to the temple to marry a wonderful girl. I want to be the best I can be for her. I need to know that I am forgiven. And I need to know now. Tell me how to find out." I said I would try.

He gave me a deadline. As I recall, it was less than two weeks away. Fortunately, during that period of time I went to Salt Lake City and found myself seeing Elder Spencer W. Kimball, then a member of the Quorum of the Twelve, at a social function. It was crowded, and yet he somehow found me. He walked up to me in that crowd and said, "Hal, I understand that you are now a bishop. Do you have anything you would like to ask me?"

I said that I did, but I didn't think that was the place to talk about it. He thought it was. It was an outdoor party. My memory is that we went behind a shrub and there had our interview. Without breaking confidences, I outlined the concerns and the question of this young man in my ward. Then I asked Elder Kimball, "How can he get that revelation? How can he know whether his sins are remitted?"

I thought Elder Kimball would talk to me about fasting or prayer or listening for the still small voice. But he surprised me. Instead he said, "Tell me something about the young man."

I said, "What would you like to know?"

And then he began a series of the most simple questions. Some of the ones I remember were:

"Does he come to his priesthood meetings?"

I said, after a moment of thought, "Yes."

"Does he come early?"

"Yes."

"Does he sit toward the front?"

I thought for a moment and then realized, to my amazement, that he did.

"Does he home teach?"

"Yes."

"Does he go early in the month?"

"Yes, he does."

"Does he go more than once?"

"Yes."

I can't remember the other questions. But they were all like that—little things, simple acts of obedience, of submission. And for each question I was surprised that my answer was always yes. Yes, he wasn't just at all his meetings: he was early; he was smiling; he was there not only with his whole heart, but with the broken heart of a little child, as he was every time the Lord asked anything of him. And after I had said yes to each of his questions, Elder Kimball looked at me, paused, and then very quietly said, "There is your revelation."

Sufficiently humble. Stripped of pride. Stripped of envy. Never making a mock of his brother.

When I went back to the young man and told him what I then knew, he accepted it. But he may have simply had to take my word for it. You see, it's hard to feel that you are sufficiently humble. If you did, you might not be. He went forward with his marriage. I've seen him since. To me he still looks as he did on the front bench before a priesthood meeting.

My guess is that he has retained a remission of his sins. I don't know if he knew then or if he knows now with the certainty he wanted, but I am sure of something. When that change of heart comes to me and to you, when we are cleansed and blameless before God, it will be because we have been made pure by the blood of Christ. And I know what I can and must do. I must be baptized by a servant of God holding the true priesthood, I must have received the gift of the Holy Ghost by that same power, and then I must have exercised faith in the Savior long enough and carefully enough that his grace will be sufficient for me. And I know at least one way to know that is happening in my life—or in yours. You will have put yourself so often in the Master's service, bringing the cleansing companionship of the Holy Ghost, that you will be on the front row, early, whenever and wherever the Master calls. It will be gradual enough that you may not notice. You will be humble enough that you may be reluctant to believe it is happening. But those with spiritual discernment who love you will know. And the Savior and our Heavenly Father will know. And that is enough.

Here is another of those scriptures from Elder Tuttle, marked in the margin. It describes an evidence you and I can have that we are on the way to that better, higher life: "For the natural man is an enemy to God, and has been from the fall of Adam, and will be, forever and ever, unless he yields to the enticings of the Holy Spirit, and putteth off the natural man and becometh a saint through the atonement of Christ the Lord, and becometh as a child, submissive, meek, humble, patient, full of love, willing to submit to all things which the Lord seeth fit to inflict upon him, even as a child doth submit to his father." (Mosiah 3:19.)

When I read that scripture I see the face of that young man on the front row, early to his meeting.

I pray that you and I will make the choices today and tomorrow and as long as we live that will bring the influence of the Holy Ghost into our lives in the service of the Master. I testify that as we do, we will feel the cleansing that comes through the Savior's atonement, and with it the confidence that we are coming unto him. And when we are there, with him and sanctified, we shall never hunger or thirst again.

My hope is that you will put yourself in the way today where the Holy Ghost will go with you. A telephone call, a visit, or a letter you could write to one or more of the people God has asked you to serve would do that. I've promised you one miracle: you will feel the companionship of the Holy Ghost. But I have to warn you about expecting another miracle. Even with the help of the Holy Ghost, you may not say the words or give the service that will bring a mighty change in their lives.

Remember that President McKay said that at "some period" in their lives they will feel an irresistible desire to rise to a higher, more beautiful world. That may not be today. But go anyway. And go again. And when the time comes for those whom you serve, you will be there, you will be their friend, and you can testify to them that the long-ing they feel for something better is to come unto Christ. You can tell them how. And you will have been showing them how.

I have one other plea, one other hope for you: don't ignore the impulses that come to you to rise above yourself into a higher and more beautiful world. Growing up, get-ting educated, seeing the world, and almost everything that happens to you will push you toward saying to yourself: "Oh, that was just a dream. That's not possible. I could never change that much."

You can. The Savior promised, "Come unto me, all ye that labour and are heavy laden, and I will give you rest." (Matthew 11:28.)

He can and he will.

I bear you my testimony that you can invite the Holy Ghost into your life, and because you have been promised that gift by authorized servants of God, he will come. I bear testimony that you can be cleansed by the power of the Atonement. The yearning you've felt for something better is a yearning to come unto Christ. This promise in section 19 of the Doctrine and Covenants is true: "Learn of me, and listen to my words; walk in the meekness of my Spirit, and you shall have peace in me." (D&C 19:23.)

I testify that God lives. He is your Father. You want to go home. You want to be with him. The only way you can do so is to become clean and spotless. I bear you my testimony that Jesus is the Christ, that the Atonement is real, and that the Holy Ghost will come to you as you go forward to serve the Lord with confidence and faith.

CHAPTER 5

CHOOSE TO BE GOOD

There is a paradox in today's world. Over the last several years manufacturers, service providers, and consumers have become increasingly quality-conscious. For instance, on the cover of a recent issue of *Business Week* appeared the word "Quality" along with this headline: "Manufacturing: The Next Goal Is Perfection." But at the very time when more and more of us are choosing quality in the products and services we create and use, a strange thing is happening: more and more people are making the opposite choice for their personal lives. They choose to design lives for themselves that put the chance of a moral failure high, coolly accepting the expectation that sin will come and apparently hoping that they can somehow take care of it easily, at little cost. There is even a phrase for that choice, borrowed from the world of cars: "Live in the fast lane."

Because those choices seem to be made consciously and seldom out of raw emotion, they must appear reasonable to the people making them. Years ago a professor of mine, Ray

---

From a talk given at a BYU Devotional, 12 November 1991.

Bauer, corrected me when I put the label of "irrational" on someone's behavior. He said: "Hal, you'll understand people better if you assume that people's behavior is rational, at least from their point of view. Try to see what they see."

Well, then, if people are choosing to make sin—moral defects—highly likely, they must see the world in a way that makes that choice reasonable. Why would people choose to put themselves in the places, listen to the sounds, see the sights, be with the people, entertain the thoughts, and do the things that will require them to face the effects of sin?

First, they might believe that there is no God, and therefore no moral law, and thus no sin. A second possibility is that they believe we are so good by nature, and God so kind, that whatever we do is right. You remember King Lamoni, the missionary contact of Ammon from the Book of Mormon? He believed that—at least he believed it at first. In Alma we read: "Now this was the tradition of Lamoni, which he had received from his father, that there was a Great Spirit. Notwithstanding they believed in a Great Spirit, they supposed that whatsoever they did was right." But even with all that tradition, Lamoni could feel the Spirit of Christ. You remember the next phrase: "Nevertheless, Lamoni began to fear exceedingly, with fear lest he had done wrong in slaying his servants." (Alma 18:5.)

A third reason to risk sin would be to believe that the Atonement makes correcting the effects of sin, even of the most terrible kind, a simple matter. There seem to be more and more people who act as if they believe that. They believe the "eat, drink, and be merry" promise. They must think easy forgiveness can come from their bishop in this life in the same way the deceivers described in 2 Nephi said it would come from God in the next life. Here is the lie, which the Book of Mormon prophesied would be told by many. I feel it is being believed by many: "And there shall also be many which shall say: Eat, drink, and be merry; nevertheless, fear God—he will justify in committing a little sin; yea, lie a little, take the advantage of one because of his words, dig a pit for thy neighbor; there is no harm in this; and do all these things, for tomorrow we die; and if it so be that we are guilty, God will beat us with a few stripes, and at last we shall be saved in the kingdom of God." (2 Nephi 28:8.)

My testimony is that the facts are contrary to each of those assumptions. First, there is a God. I testify to you that the Prophet Joseph Smith was accurately describing God and sin with these words:

> And now, after the many testimonies which have been given of him, this is the testimony, last of all, which we give of him: That he lives!
>
> For we saw him, even on the right hand of God; and we heard the voice bearing record that he is the Only Begotten of the Father—
>
> That by him, and through him, and of him, the worlds are and were created, and the inhabitants thereof are begotten sons and daughters unto God.
>
> And this we saw also, and bear record, that an angel of God who was in authority in the presence of God, who rebelled against the Only Begotten Son whom the Father loved and who was in the bosom of the Father, was thrust down from the presence of God and the Son,
>
> And was called Perdition, for the heavens wept over him—he was Lucifer, a son of the morning. (D&C 76:22–26.)

And then these chilling words in verse 29: "Wherefore, he maketh war with the saints of God, and encompasseth them round about."

I further testify that even God, with all his power and with all his love, cannot take us home to live with him again if we are unclean. You, and I, and all of our Father's children will someday know that being with God is being home—and that everywhere else, however beautiful it may be, will be a place where you long for home. Here is a description of the terrible fact that our Father in Heaven cannot let us be with him again without our being washed clean:

> Wherefore, if they should die in their wickedness they must be cast off also, as to the things which are spiritual, which are pertaining to righteousness; wherefore, they must be brought to stand before God, to be judged of their works; and if their works have been filthiness they must needs be filthy; and if they be filthy it must needs be that they cannot dwell in the kingdom of God; if so, the kingdom of God must be filthy also. But behold, I say unto you, the kingdom of God is not filthy, and there cannot any unclean thing enter into the kingdom of God; wherefore there must needs be a place of filthiness prepared for that which is filthy. (1 Nephi 15:33–34.)

This is my warning to you today. It is a bad estimate of your personal costs to believe that a choice to commit sin is made so free by the power of the Atonement that we can have painless forgiveness. President Spencer W. Kimball said:

> To every forgiveness there is a condition. The plaster must be as wide as the sore. The fasting, the prayers, the humility must be equal to or greater than the sin. There must be a broken heart and a contrite spirit. There must be "sackcloth and ashes." There must be tears and genuine change of heart. There must be conviction of the sin, abandonment of the evil, confession of the error to properly constituted authorities of the Lord. There must be restitution and a confirmed,

determined change of pace, direction and destination. Conditions must be controlled and companionship corrected or changed. There must be a washing of robes to get them white and there must be a new consecration and devotion to the living of all of the laws of God. In short, there must be an overcoming of self, of sin, and of the world. (*The Miracle of Forgiveness*, p. 353.)

That is not a description of an easy fix justifying a purposely flawed life. That is not a description of a "few stripes." How much better to choose to be good and to do it early, a long way upstream from the terrible effects of sin.

Upon hearing President Kimball's description of the effort repentance requires, those who are now in serious sin will have a thought delivered to their minds that goes something like this: "Well, if it is that difficult to repent, I might as well go on in sin. Later, when I need forgiveness, I'll just go through that once."

That is so unwise. Let me tell you why. First, people who postpone repentance may run out of time. And second, they will find more misery in more sin, not the happiness they hope for but can't find. Remember the warning from Samuel the Lamanite: "But behold, your days of probation are past; ye have procrastinated the day of your salvation until it is everlastingly too late, and your destruction is made sure; yea, for ye have sought all the days of your lives for that which ye could not obtain; and ye have sought for happiness in doing iniquity, which thing is contrary to the nature of that righteousness which is in our great and Eternal Head." (Helaman 13:38.)

If you've avoided serious sin, you may be thinking, "None of this applies to me." But it does. The choice to be good is the same and is equally necessary for every person. The choice to be good, which is what repentance includes, must be made by all of us. It is more difficult and more

65

urgent for those in serious sin, but these words apply to everyone: "And the days of the children of men were prolonged, according to the will of God, that they might repent while in the flesh; wherefore, their state became a state of probation, and their time was lengthened, according to the commandments which the Lord God gave unto the children of men. For he gave commandment that all men must repent; for he showed unto all men that they were lost, because of the transgression of their parents." (2 Nephi 2:21.)

I know I don't need to persuade you to choose to be good. The fact that you're reading this book is pretty fair evidence that you want to make a lasting choice to be good. But the fact is that most of us have made that choice more than once. We're a little like some of the companies who have made a commitment, a serious choice, to pursue quality. Somehow, after a vigorous start, the effort peters out.

Since I've had that experience, too, of fading resolutions to be good, I've thought some about why it happens. The problem is this: We all need a standard, something to compare our behavior with, to help us decide what a practical goal of goodness is. And most of us choose people to compare ourselves with. I learned long ago that it matters who you choose for that comparison. Let me tell you how I learned.

Years ago, before adolescence hit me, I read a book called *Gospel Ideals*. It was a collection of excerpts from the talks of President David O. McKay. One chapter described how you would know when you were in love and, therefore, how you should view and treat women. President McKay's lofty words more than touched my heart: I felt a confirmation that they were true. Without telling anyone, I took his words as one of my standards of goodness.

Five or six years later, I was playing basketball with a

66

very fine team in a league in the city where I lived. Our team was composed of returned missionaries plus me, the kid. Up to that point, I had never had a date. And I had no sisters, so what I thought I knew about girls and how to treat them came mostly from the visions I got from *Gospel Ideals*. I remember riding home one night from a game with those returned missionaries. I sat in the back seat of the car, and they talked about girls. I remember that as I listened to them, the thought came into my mind: "I have been wrong. Those ideals about girls and how you should feel about them, how you should treat them, they are unrealistic."

Luckily, in a few years I learned that they were wrong and President McKay was right. Or perhaps, in fairness to those young men, I learned that the things I *thought* they had said were not the true standard of goodness. But, you see, that's the problem with using people as your standard or your guide—they may be wrong, or you may be unable to discern what they really think and what they really do.

That is particularly true about the best of people. You see, the Lord said, "Do not your alms before men." (Matthew 6:1.) And the best people don't. They do good very privately. Now and then I get a glimpse, always by accident, of the way some people live the simple commandments of the gospel of Jesus Christ. They don't know more than you and I know; they just do more of the simple things you and I have already been taught as children in a Primary class. I discover acts of kindness, of forgiveness, or of moral endurance beyond what I had thought we could do. And when those invisible lives become visible to me for a moment, a fear runs through me and with it the thought: "Maybe what I thought was good enough, when I get to the other side, won't be. Maybe some humble people—maybe lots of them—are living better than I thought I could."

67

That underlines for me again the risk in taking my standards from other people.

But in this struggle to use people as our guide to what is good enough, I've found this clue: the best guides, the safest source of standards, have always been the people called by God to lead me. As I've told you, one of the lodestars of my life came from a book by President David O. McKay. I've noticed that the truest guides have been prophets and parents and bishops and teachers—good people called of God to help me. And while sometimes the Spirit has told me to use their lives as guides, more often it has been to set my course by their inspired words.

The reason for that, it seems to me, is that the only safe standard to guide our choice to be good is God. Those who can speak for him, under authority, are holding up the true standard of goodness. God told us that in this way: "Old things are done away, and all things have become new. Therefore I would that ye should be perfect even as I, or your Father who is in heaven is perfect." (3 Nephi 12:47–48.)

You might well object by saying that human examples are so much more accessible for observation. No, humans are more available, but, at least in my experience, their lives are not more accessible. Our Father in Heaven and the Savior have revealed themselves in detail through prophets, through heavenly visitations, and in person since man was created. There is a clearer description of the goodness of God than you will get of any mortal you can observe.

And you need not fear that using God as your standard will overwhelm you. On the contrary—God asks only that we approach him humbly, as a child. He does not require that we master some difficult doctrine. A child can enter the kingdom of heaven. Remember the description of that surrender in the Book of Mormon: "For the natural man is an enemy to God, and has been from the fall of Adam, and will be, forever and ever, unless he yields to the enticings of the Holy Spirit, and putteth off the natural man and becometh a saint through the atonement of Christ the Lord, and becometh as a child, submissive, meek, humble, patient, full of love, willing to submit to all things which the Lord seeth fit to inflict upon him, even as a child doth submit to his father." (Mosiah 3:19.)

That submission, that simple desire to do what he would have us do, makes available to you and me the sure guide for knowing what is good. If you want to believe in Christ, if you want to do good, the Spirit of Christ and the Holy Ghost will prompt you. Here is the promise: "For behold, my brethren, it is given unto you to judge, that ye may know good from evil; and the way to judge is as plain, that ye may know with a perfect knowledge, as the daylight is from the dark night. For behold, the Spirit of Christ is given to every man, that he may know good from evil; wherefore, I show unto you the way to judge; for every thing which inviteth to do good, and to persuade to believe in Christ, is sent forth by the power and gift of Christ; wherefore ye may know with a perfect knowledge it is of God." (Moroni 7:15–16.)

Two ways of applying that invitation to be guided have worked for me. One is to read the scriptures to try to feel what the Savior feels. For me, that happens most often when I read the description of the resurrected Savior among the Nephites. Here is a single verse that helps me: "And it came to pass that when they had knelt upon the ground, Jesus groaned within himself, and said: Father, I am troubled because of the wickedness of the people of the house of Israel." (3 Nephi 17:14.)

Now, for me, at the right moment, I can begin to feel the pain the Savior felt for sins, yours and mine. His groan

69

within himself came after he had paid the price for us, after the Atonement. His being troubled was not some abstract grief for our sins and those of the house of Israel. His was real pain, recently felt, as he took upon him the sins of the world. I can't experience that, but I can sense it enough to have sorrow for what I have added to it. I can resolve to add no more. And I can feel determination that I will help offer the full blessings of the Atonement to as many as I can, because that passage helps me feel, in a small way, what taking upon him the sins of all mankind cost the Savior.

As I try to feel what he felt, I've tried to do another thing, both as I read and in prayer: I've tried to know what he would do if he had my opportunities. You might try that. If you have had trouble getting answers to your prayers, try asking today, "What is there that you would have me do?" That prayer will be answered if you are sincere and if you listen like a little child, with real intent to act.

I must be careful about what I promise you as you try choosing to be good. It won't be all roses. President Ezra Taft Benson spent a lifetime trying to be good. Every time I was with him I felt his goodness. As nearly as I could tell, he had used the Savior as his standard about as well as anyone I ever knew. And yet, in his advanced years, life got harder, not easier. In 1989 he expressed a sense of joy that included the edge of reality: "I leave you my testimony of the joy of living—of the joys of *full* gospel living and of going through the Refiner's fire and the sanctification process that takes place. As the Apostle Paul so well said, 'We know that all things work together for good to them that love God.' (Romans 8:28.)" ("To the Elderly of the Church," *Ensign*, November 1989, p. 8.)

A choice to be good—even with the trials that come— will allow the Atonement to change your heart. In time and after persistence, your wants and even your needs will change. You remember that the people who believed King Benjamin's talk found such a change had come to them: "And they all cried with one voice, saying: Yea, we believe all the words which thou hast spoken unto us; and also, we know of their surety and truth, because of the Spirit of the Lord Omnipotent, which has wrought a mighty change in us, or in our hearts, that we have no more disposition to do evil, but to do good continually." (Mosiah 5:2.)

If we stay at it long enough, perhaps for a lifetime, we will have for so long felt what the Savior feels, wanted what he wants, and done what he would have us do that we will have, through the Atonement, a new heart filled with charity. And we will have become like him. That promise also is in the Book of Mormon: "Charity is the pure love of Christ, and it endureth forever; and whoso is found possessed of it at the last day, it shall be well with him. Wherefore, my beloved brethren, pray unto the Father with all the energy of heart, that ye may be filled with this love, which he hath bestowed upon all who are true followers of his Son, Jesus Christ; that ye may become the sons of God; that when he shall appear we shall be like him, for we shall see him as he is; that we may have this hope; that we may be purified even as he is pure. Amen." (Moroni 7:47–48.)

You can make the choice to be good early. You can use the Savior as your standard for goodness. And you can stay with it. President Benson gave us that assurance, and I testify that it is true. He said: "Attaining a righteous and virtuous life is within the capability of any one of us if we will earnestly seek for it. If we do not have these character traits, the Lord has told us that we should 'ask, and ye shall receive; knock, and it shall be opened unto you.' (D&C 4:7.) The Apostle Peter tells us that when we possess these traits we are not 'unfruitful in the *knowledge* of our Lord Jesus Christ.' (2 Peter 1:8; emphasis added.) To know the

Savior, then, is to be *like* Him. God will bless us to be like His Son when we make an earnest effort." ("What Manner of Men Ought We to Be?" *Ensign*, November 1983, p. 43.)

I add my testimony that God the Father lives, that we will want to be with him forever, that eternal life requires that we be clean, without spot, and that the Atonement of Jesus Christ and the restoration of the keys to the earth through the Prophet Joseph Smith make that possible. I pray that we will choose to be good, take the Savior as our standard, and make the earnest effort, persistently, however difficult the way, until we may someday see him and find that we have become like him.

CHAPTER 6

REMEMBRANCE AND GRATITUDE

Many of you have had the same experience I have had. And if you haven't, you will. You will go to a hospital or to a house to comfort someone, and instead he or she comforts you. Or you try to encourage someone who seems to you to have so little, and yet he or she expresses gratitude for things you take for granted.

To find gratitude and generosity when you could reasonably find hurt and resentment will surprise you. It will be so surprising because you will see so much of the opposite: people who have much more than others yet who react with anger when one advantage is lost or with resentment when an added gift is denied.

A poem describes that contrast: it is called "How Different."

> *Some murmur when the sky is clear*
> *And wholly bright to view,*
> *If one small speck of dark appear*

From a talk given at General Conference, 30 September 1989.

73

In their great heaven of blue:
And some with thankful love are filled,
If but one streak of light,
One ray of God's good mercy, gild
The darkness of their night.
(Richard Chenevix Trench, in Sourcebook of
Poetry *[Grand Rapids, Mich.: Zondervan*
Publishing House, 1968], p. 396.)

You and I would like to know how to control our wants and increase our gratitude and generosity. We are going to need that change. Someday, in our families and as a people, we will live as one, seeking each other's good.

You know from studying Church history that we have tried to live as one in a variety of settings. A story from one of those tries, in Orderville, Utah, gives us a clue as to why it is so hard.

Orderville was founded in 1870 and 1871 by people who wanted to live the united order; in 1875, they began the order. They built housing units in a square, with a common dining hall. They built a storehouse, shoe shop, bakery, blacksmith shop, tannery, schoolhouse, sheep shed, and woolen factory. They grew and made nearly everything they needed, from soap to trousers. They had carpenters, midwives, teachers, artists, and musicians. They produced enough surplus that they could sell it in neighboring towns for cash; with that they built up a capital fund to buy more land and equipment.

The population rose to seven hundred people. One hundred and fifty of them gave Orderville a special advantage: they had come to Orderville from the mission on the Muddy River, where they had nearly starved. When those who had been called to the Muddy were released, they were in near destitution. More than twenty of those families went to Long Valley, founded Orderville, and pledged all they had to the Lord. They didn't have much, but their poverty may have been their greatest contribution. Their having almost nothing provided a basis for future comparison that might have guaranteed gratitude; any food or clothing or housing that came to them in Orderville would be treasure compared to their privation on the Muddy mission.

But time passed, the railroad came, and a mining boom put cash in the hands of people in the neighboring towns. They could buy imported clothes, and they did. The people in Orderville were living better than they had in years, but the memory of poverty on the Muddy may have faded. They now focused on what was in the next town. And so they felt old-fashioned and deprived.

One ingenious boy acted on the discontent he felt when he was denied a new pair of pants from the Orderville factory because his were not worn out yet. He secretly gathered the docked lambs' tails from the spring crop. He sheared the wool from them and stored it in sacks. Then, when he was sent with a load of wool to sell in Nephi, he took his sacks along and exchanged them for a pair of store pants. He created a sensation when he wore the new-style pants to the next dance.

The president of the order asked him what he had done. The boy gave an honest answer. So they called him into a meeting and told him to bring the pants. They commended him for his initiative, pointed out that the pants really belonged to the order, and took them. But they told him this: the pants would be taken apart, used as a pattern, and henceforth Orderville pants would have the new store-bought style. And he would get the first pair.

That did not quite end the pants rebellion. Orders for new pants soon swamped the tailoring department. When the orders were denied because pants weren't yet worn out, boys began slipping into the shed where the grinding wheel was housed. Soon, pants began to wear out quickly. The elders gave in, sent a load of wool out to trade for cloth, and the new-style pants were produced for everyone.

There were many challenges Orderville faced in the ten years they lived the order there. One of them they never really conquered is one with which we all struggle. It was the problem of not remembering. That is a problem we must solve, too.

Just as the memory of poverty would fade, we so easily forget that we came into life with nothing. Whatever we get soon seems our natural right, not a gift. And we forget the giver. Then our gaze shifts from what we have been given to what we don't have yet.

God has used one method over and over to help with that problem of remembering. A group of people in the Book of Mormon record lost their flocks, their herds, and their fields of grain. Some lost their lives. And then the survivors remembered. In Alma it says, "And so great were their afflictions that every soul had cause to mourn; and they believed that it was the judgments of God sent upon them because of their wickedness and their abominations; therefore they were awakened to a remembrance of their duty." (Alma 4:3.)

Confronting death and difficulty does return memory and therefore gratitude to righteous people as well as the wicked. But there must be another, a better, way to remember, one we can choose.

There is. A servant of God named King Benjamin taught it to his people and to us.

He taught them that none of us was above another because we are all dust, to which God has given life and then sustained it. He described a fact which is true for every human being: unforgiven sin will bring us unending torment. And he described the gift we all have been offered: those whose faith in Jesus Christ leads them to repentance and forgiveness will live in never-ending happiness.

King Benjamin's teaching had a miraculous effect. Gratitude for what they had led to faith unto repentance. That led to forgiveness. That produced new gratitude. And then King Benjamin taught that, if we can remember and so remain grateful, we will retain a remission of our sins through all the losses and the gains of life. He taught it this way:

> And again I say unto you as I have said before, that as ye have come to the knowledge of the glory of God, or if ye have known of his goodness and have tasted of his love, and have received a remission of your sins, which causeth such exceedingly great joy in your souls, even so I would that ye should remember, and always retain in remembrance, the greatness of God, and your own nothingness, and his goodness and long-suffering towards you, unworthy creatures, and humble yourselves even in the depths of humility, calling on the name of the Lord daily, and standing steadfastly in the faith of that which is to come, which was spoken by the mouth of the angel.
>
> And behold, I say unto you that if ye do this ye shall always rejoice, and be filled with the love of God, and always retain a remission of your sins; and ye shall grow in the knowledge of the glory of him that created you, or in the knowledge of that which is just and true. (Mosiah 4:11–12.)

How can you and I remember, always, the goodness of God, that we can retain a remission of our sins? The Apostle John recorded what the Savior taught us of a gift of remembrance which comes through the gift of the Holy Ghost: "But the Comforter, which is the Holy Ghost, whom the Father will send in my name, he shall teach you all things, and bring all things to your remembrance, what-soever I have said unto you." (John 14:26.)

The Holy Ghost brings back memories of what God has taught us. And one of the ways God teaches us is with his blessings; and so, if we choose to exercise faith, the Holy Ghost will bring God's kindnesses to our remembrance.

You could test that in prayer today. You could follow the command, "Thou shalt thank the Lord thy God in all things." (D&C 59:7.) President Ezra Taft Benson suggested prayer as a time to do that. He said: "The Prophet Joseph said at one time that one of the greatest sins of which the Latter-day Saints would be guilty is the sin of ingratitude. I presume most of us have not thought of that as a great sin. There is a great tendency for us in our prayers and in our pleadings with the Lord to ask for additional blessings. But sometimes I feel we need to devote more of our prayers to expressions of gratitude and thanksgiving for blessings already received. We enjoy so much." (*God, Family, Country: Our Three Great Loyalties* [Salt Lake City: Deseret Book Co., 1974], p. 199.)

You could have an experience with the gift of the Holy Ghost today. You could begin a private prayer with thanks. You could start to count your blessings and then pause for a moment. If you exercise faith, and with the gift of the Holy Ghost, you will find that memories of other blessings will flood into your mind. If you begin to express gratitude for each of them, your prayer may take a little longer than usual. Remembrance will come. And so will gratitude.

You could try the same thing as you write an entry in your book of remembrance. The Holy Ghost has helped with that since the beginning of time. You remember in the record of Moses it says, "And a book of remembrance was kept, in the which was recorded, in the language of Adam, for it was given unto as many as called upon God to write by the spirit of inspiration." (Moses 6:5.)

President Spencer W. Kimball described that process of inspired writing: "Those who keep a book of remembrance are more likely to keep the Lord in remembrance in their daily lives. Journals are a way of counting our blessings and of leaving an inventory of these blessings for our posterity." (*The Teachings of Spencer W. Kimball,* p. 349.)

As you start to write, you could ask yourself, "How did God bless me today?" If you do that long enough and with faith, you will find yourself remembering blessings. And sometimes you will have gifts brought to your mind which you failed to notice during the day, but which you will then know were a touch of God's hand in your life.

You can choose to remember the greatest gift of all. Next week you can go to a meeting where the sacrament is administered. You will hear the words, "Always remember him." You can pledge to do that, and the Holy Ghost will help you. President Marion G. Romney talked about the gift we will be helped to remember. He said: "We should be thankful and express appreciation for all favors received—and surely we receive many. The chief objects of our gratitude, however, should be, and are, God, our Heavenly Father, and his son Jesus Christ, our Lord and Redeemer. . . . To the Lord Jesus we owe an undying debt of gratitude, for he bought us with a great price. It is impossible for us, weak mortals as we are, to fully comprehend and appreciate the sufferings he endured on the cross that he might gain for us the victory over death." ("'Thou Shalt Thank the Lord Thy God in All Things,'" *Ensign,* June 1974, p. 3.)

I bear you my testimony that Jesus is the Christ, that he atoned for our sins, and that the keys which unlock the doors of eternal life were restored to the Prophet Joseph Smith and are on the earth today.

Not long ago a man asked me, "Does your church still believe that when Christ comes you will be living as one, the way they did in the city of Enoch?" He put a spin on the word *still*, as if we might not believe such a thing anymore. I said, "Yes, we do." And then he said, "You are the people who could do it."

I do not know why he thought that, but I know why he was right. He was right because this is the kingdom of God. Your baptism for the remission of sins and your receiving the gift of the Holy Ghost were offered by priesthood servants recognized by God.

And so the remembrance King Benjamin urged upon us can be ours. Remembrance is the seed of gratitude, which is the seed of generosity. Gratitude for the remission of sins is the seed of charity, the pure love of Christ. And so God has made possible for you and me this blessing, a change in our very natures: "And the remission of sins bringeth meekness, and lowliness of heart; and because of meekness and lowliness of heart cometh the visitation of the Holy Ghost, which Comforter filleth with hope and perfect love, which love endureth by diligence unto prayer, until the end shall come, when all the saints shall dwell with God." (Moroni 8:26.)

I pray that we may make the simple choices which will lead us there to dwell with Him. And I pray that we will remember and be grateful for the gift of the Atonement and the gift of the Holy Ghost, which make that journey possible.

CHAPTER 7

TRIALS OF FAITH

I'd like to tell you a little bit about what I think your future will be like. When I meet old friends or former students and ask them about their experiences since the last time we were together, they almost always say they've been surprised—that is, things haven't turned out quite the way they had expected. They thought they were going to live in a certain place or follow a certain career, and something else happened instead. In some cases they talk about it with tears because it's been hard, in other cases with smiles because it's been funny. But they often seem to feel that life has been full of surprises.

I think of a scripture in Ecclesiastes: "The race is not to the swift, nor the battle to the strong, neither yet bread to the wise, nor yet riches to men of understanding, nor yet favour to men of skill; but time and chance happeneth to them all." (Ecclesiastes 9:11.) One of the toughest things about the idea of chance is that it can discourage people. And I'll tell you something else that worries me. If people believe that life is all surprises, at least a few are going to

---

From a talk given at a Ricks College Devotional, 16 February 1988.

say, "Why bother to prepare for what's ahead? I never know what's going to happen anyway. Whatever comes, I'll just let it come."

I had a daydream as I grew up. I used to have real trouble hitting pitches in baseball, particularly when the guys got old enough that they knew how to throw curves. And I remember having a fantasy that I could be a great hitter if I just knew where the next pitch was going to be— just let me know where it is and I'll hit it. And your life is going to be like that sometimes; there are going to be some surprises, which you wish you could anticipate.

But there's something else. There are some certainties. And I'd like to tell you about three certainties, things that you can prepare for with the absolute assurance that your preparations won't be wasted. Some of this I know from my own life, some of it from talking with others. But much of it is from the scriptures, and much of it you already know to be true through the whisperings of the Holy Ghost.

Now, be very careful when anybody tells you about certainty in this world, because it's a very uncertain life. In fact, most of us are so worried about the fact that we don't know what's coming that we're easy prey for people who claim to be able to tell us exactly what's going to happen to us. Do you remember a man named Nehor in the Book of Mormon? He wanted to become popular and wealthy, so he preached a message that he knew people would like. He essentially said, "I'll tell you something about the future that's certain, and I'll make it very attractive." The scriptures record that he "testified unto the people that all mankind should be saved at the last day, and that they need not fear nor tremble, but that they might lift up their heads and rejoice; for the Lord had created all men, and had also redeemed all men; and, in the end, all men should have eternal life." (Alma 1:4.) And many of the people believed him. If they had searched the scriptures and prayed about his message, they would have known it was a lie. But he told them a pleasant lie—don't worry, all will go well—and many believed him.

I remind you of that story for two reasons. One is that as you read this discussion about what I say is certain in your future, you need to have the Holy Ghost tell you that what I'm saying is true. The other reason is that you need to read the scriptures I'll share with you, study them in their full context, and see if they confirm what I'm going to tell you.

Now, what I'm going to do is suggest three things that are certain to happen to you in the future. First, it is an absolute certainty that you will go through trials of your faith. For some it will be a physical or a perhaps a financial problem. For others it may not be anything that an outsider would see as a trial. But the real trial of your faith is not necessarily that moment when disaster obviously strikes you; in fact, you may go through a lifetime with little or almost none of that. The real trial of your faith is anything that would divert you from doing what God would have you do.

I'm thinking of a young man I spoke with a few years ago in a city in California. I was meeting with him because he and his wife were having great difficulties. At first I couldn't sense what the problem was, but later he told me he thought it grew out of his employment. He was working in a law enforcement activity that required him to do some things that kept him both away from his family and away from his church work. He saw no way he could do anything other than that, and yet he quietly said to me that he knew there had been a change in his life. By not being able to do the little things that God had asked of him, he had felt a lessening of his faith.

You can be absolutely assured that in one form or another there will come a trial of your faith. And I would hope you wouldn't be surprised. The Apostle Peter said, "Beloved, think it not strange concerning the fiery trial which is to try you, as though some strange thing happened unto you: but rejoice, inasmuch as ye are partakers of Christ's sufferings; that, when his glory shall be revealed, you may be glad also with exceeding joy." (1 Peter 4:12–13.)

One of the reasons why you will be tried is that opposition is always part of being a faithful member of The Church of Jesus Christ of Latter-day Saints. You should expect that great difficulties will come to you in the pursuit of doing what the Lord would have you do. But you should also feel that these trials are a blessing, because "faith is things which are hoped for and not seen; wherefore, dispute not because ye see not, for ye receive no witness until after the trial of your faith." (Ether 12:6.)

I'd like to suggest something about how to receive through our trials the blessing that's promised in that scripture. Perhaps you're being tried right now, and you may feel like saying to me, "Well, Brother Eyring, it's pretty tough right now. Do you mean this is going to go on over a lifetime?" And my answer is yes. It will be intermittent; there will be times when things go very badly, and there will be times when you think things are going wonderfully well. (If you'll remember my definition of a trial, you'll want to be careful about the times when things seem to be going well.) But the trials will continue to come.

One time when I was serving in the Presiding Bishopric, I had a remarkable week during which we were dealing with a series of tough problems. I met with the First Presidency four or five times during that week, and in each meeting I was supposed to suggest answers to some very, very hard problems. In every instance I felt the hand of heaven touch me and guide me so that I knew what to say. In one case the First Presidency even confirmed that my proposed solution was what needed to be done. That's a wonderful feeling, and I started thinking that things were rolling along pretty well in my life.

Then I came home, and my wife and I got into a conversation about some problem that she and I were working on at that time. During the conversation I expressed my opinion a little too forcefully, as if I knew the answer and there didn't need to be a lot more discussion. I immediately felt the Holy Ghost leave the room. I was about to leave for a stake conference, and I was almost frightened because I knew I could do no good without the Lord's help. So on that stake conference trip I began to analyze what had gone wrong, and I suddenly realized that you can have a trial of your faith from success. I had thought that I was doing wonderfully well, and that led me to act as if I were someone special—to act in a way that grieved the Holy Ghost.

If you'll remember that the key to not being diverted from serving God is humility, then you'll understand that some of those days when you thought things were going badly were a great blessing. You might not have sought them, but if you react to such days by recognizing your dependence on God, you could actually be in a better situation than if everything had gone extremely well. Too much success, in fact, could lead you into a more difficult trial because it could make you arrogant.

To hear the voice of the Holy Ghost requires a humble and a meek heart. Although it may sometimes feel like chastisement when life gets difficult, remember that the scriptures tell us, "Verily, thus saith the Lord unto you whom I love, and whom I love I also chasten that their sins may be forgiven, for with the chastisement I prepare a way for their deliverance in all things out of temptation, and I have loved you—wherefore, ye must needs be chastened and stand rebuked before my face." (D&C 95:1–2.) That doesn't sound so strange after you've thought about it. Our Father in Heaven loves us; he wants us to be guided, and he knows we can't be guided in arrogance. So when you're enduring what seems to be a trial or a test, when things don't seem to be going well, you can know that you have a loving Father who is allowing you to have experiences that can bless you.

When you're experiencing a severe trial, ask yourself this question: "Am I trying to do what the Lord would have me do?" If you're not, then adjust your course. But if you are, remember the boy outside the walls of Jerusalem who turned to his brothers and said, "I will go and do the things which the Lord hath commanded, for I know that the Lord giveth no commandments unto the children of men, save he shall prepare a way for them that they may accomplish the thing which he commandeth them." (1 Nephi 3:7.)

I bear you my testimony that the Lord will always prepare a way for you to escape from the trials you will be given if you understand two things. One is that you need to be on the Lord's errand. The second thing you need to understand is that the escape will almost never be *out* of the trial; it will usually be *through* it. If you pray to have the experience removed altogether, you may not find the way prepared for you. Instead, you need to pray to find the way of deliverance through it. Let me remind you of a beautiful story. One day the prophet Alma encountered a group of people who were going through terrible trials. When he saw how beaten down they were, "he beheld with great joy; for he beheld that their afflictions had truly humbled them, and that they were in a preparation to hear the word." (Alma 32:6.)

Now, if your afflictions truly humble you, then you see

that you're in a position to have the Holy Ghost whisper to you—not the way to have your difficulties taken from you, but the way to go through them on your errand for the Lord. If you will be humble and ask God what to do, I promise you that he will always prepare a way for your deliverance.

A second thing is certain to happen to you in the future. You will be given the opportunity to serve people who are very different from you. Some time ago someone did a survey which found that, in an average ward of the Church in the United States, there are fifty people who have some kind of handicap severe enough that they feel different and they feel hampered in coming into the meeting.

You live, or will live, with people who feel very different from you. Just the growth of the Church itself will require it, because the gospel of Jesus Christ is going to every nation, kindred, tongue, and people. They will flock to its standard, they will accept the restored gospel, and they will move and you will move. You'll find yourself in situations where those who have come into the gospel have had very different experiences than you have had. And you'll find a need to serve them.

Let me suggest a preparation that you can begin now. I even tried it recently myself, to be sure it still worked, and it does. Not long ago, early in the morning, my wife and I were in a hurry, getting ready to go somewhere. We were both under pressure, and I was pretty much turned inward toward myself, but I thought a thought. It's the thought I'd suggest you try: "Everything I have that's good is a gift from God. How would he have me use my gifts to serve someone?" And I simply asked my wife if there was anything I could do for her. It turned out that there was—I made the bed. It was such a small thing that I'm sure it doesn't sound very impressive to you, and it probably wasn't very impressive to her either. I could have done more. But as I did that simple little thing, I felt something that I've felt before. When I gave of my time in a way I thought the Savior would want me to for my wife, not only did my love for her increase—I also felt *his* love for her.

I promise you that if you'll use your gifts to serve someone else, you'll feel the Lord's love for that person. You'll also feel his love for you. And you'll be preparing for times when you will be called to serve people and to love them.

There is one more thing that is certain to happen in your future: someday you will see the face of the Savior. All of us will someday see his face when we stand before him to be judged. In Mosiah we read: "Yea, every knee shall bow, and every tongue confess before him. Yea, even at the last day, when all men shall stand to be judged of him, then shall they confess that he is God; then shall they confess, who live without God in the world, that the judgment of an everlasting punishment is just upon them; and they shall quake, and tremble, and shrink beneath the glance of his all-searching eye." (Mosiah 27:31.)

Your life will be full of surprises, and you can expect some trials. But you can also expect deliverance. You can know that God will answer your prayers and help you, so you don't need to be afraid of those trials anymore. And as you use your gifts from him to serve others, you can feel his love for them, and you can begin to love them as well.

There is a God, and he has an all-seeing eye. He can see you now, and he loves you. As you get older, you'll worry more and more about this question: "When I see him, will he smile?" You can go through this life with a picture in your mind of the Savior smiling at you. You can feel peace and happiness by seeking spiritual experiences that will bring you closer to him. The book of Helaman describes a group of people who were suffering terrible persecution but were at peace in their hearts. This is how they did it: "They did fast and pray oft, and did wax stronger and stronger in their humility, and firmer and firmer in the faith of Christ, unto the filling their souls with joy and consolation, yea, even to the purifying and the sanctification of their hearts, which sanctification cometh because of their yielding their hearts unto God." (Helaman 3:35.)

Yield your heart unto God. Ask him what it is he would have you do. Know that he will have prepared a way for you to do it, even under great difficulties. Ask him how he would have you share what you have with others, and you will feel his love. He lives and he loves you. He wants you to come home again.

Years ago, a young man I had been working with said something like this to me: "Brother Eyring, why don't you leave me alone? I don't want to go where you want to go. I don't want to have celestial life. I've got my friends. You keep telling me that if I keep going the way I'm going, I'll end up with my friends. Well, that's just fine with me." I thought for a moment, and then I asked him, "Do you ever feel lonely?" He said that he did, and I asked him to tell me about the last time he had felt lonely. He said, "I was at a party just the other night with my friends, and in the middle of the party I felt lonely." I asked him how that could be when he claimed to be so happy with his friends. He said that while he was at the party, something came into his mind. He remembered sitting on his mother's lap as a little boy, her arms around him. He remembered how he had felt compared to the way he felt then in the midst of his friends, and he felt lonely. Then I said to him, "You think you don't want a celestial life, but yes you do, because the only place in the life to come where there will be families is in the highest degree of the celestial kingdom. That will be the one place you will be able to have that feeling of being in a loving family again."

There is a God, he loves you, and he wants you home again. But that can't happen unless the gospel of Jesus Christ works in your life. You have to become purified and sanctified to go there. Please find out what it is the Lord would have you do, believe he has prepared a way for you to do it, and share what he's given you with others. As you do that, you will feel his love and you will become more like him. You will find joy and consolation, you will become sanctified by the gospel, and then you can go home again. I pray with my whole heart that I will see you there. I pray that we will both be smiling, and that we will see smiling at us the faces of our loving Heavenly Father and our Savior. If we will faithfully keep our covenants, preparing a little bit every day for the tests that will come and then meeting them with faith and humility, that great blessing will be ours.

CHAPTER 8

WAITING UPON
THE LORD

Throughout your life you will be in situations where you will want to know how to bring down the powers of heaven. I believe you can do that by waiting upon the Lord.

You and I struggle to bring down the powers of heaven. You may not think about it much, but sometimes you do. You go along on your own and then, suddenly, that's not enough. Something dramatic may happen, like having a friend or family member who needs a blessing. Or perhaps something dramatic doesn't happen; you realize that you've been teaching your class or visiting the people who have been assigned to your care with no visible effect. That may make you doubt yourself or the person who called you, or even whether you have the power to reach God.

Now, my worry is not about your testimony. You have probably had spiritual experiences and even recognized them. You may even have had remarkable spiritual experiences. But what I worry about is a fact put bluntly once by a President of the Church. It was true when he said it, and it

From a talk given at a BYU Fireside, 30 September 1990.

still is. His name was Heber J. Grant, and this is what he said: "There is but one path of safety to the Latter-day Saints, and that is the path of duty. It is not testimony, it is not marvelous manifestations, it is not knowing that the Gospel of Jesus Christ is true, . . . it is not actually knowing that the Savior is the Redeemer, and that Joseph Smith was His prophet, that will save you and me, but it is the keeping of the commandments of God, the living the life of a Latter-day Saint." (*Improvement Era,* November 1936, p. 659.)

You and I know that the path of duty and living the life of a Latter-day Saint require our bringing down the powers of heaven. Think about the duties that really matter to a Latter-day Saint: rearing children in a world of wickedness; caring for the poor when you have trouble just caring for yourselves; being a witness for the Savior wherever you may be, in whatever circumstances. You remember how Alma described the covenant we made at the waters of baptism:

> And now, as ye are desirous to come into the fold of God, and to be called his people, and are willing to bear one another's burdens, that they may be light;
>
> Yea, and are willing to mourn with those that mourn; yea, and comfort those that stand in need of comfort, and to stand as witnesses of God at all times and in all things, and in all places that ye may be in, even until death, that ye may be redeemed of God, and be numbered with those of the first resurrection, that ye may have eternal life—
>
> Now I say unto you, if this be the desire of your hearts, what have you against being baptized in the name of the Lord, as a witness before him that ye have entered into a covenant with him, that ye will serve him and keep his commandments, that he may pour out his Spirit more abundantly upon you? (Mosiah 18:8–10.)

In our more thoughtful times, you and I realize that the

promise of serving so that he may pour out his Spirit more abundantly upon us is more than a nice reward; it is a necessity. For what matters, our own power is not enough. You know that getting help won't be easy or automatic.

Let me tell you a true story, from my life, that will likely strike a chord in your memories of your own spiritual life.

Years ago I was asked to chair a committee of faculty from Brigham Young University and other schools with this question to study: What should be the future of higher education in the Church? Elder Neal A. Maxwell was then the commissioner of education. I told him I didn't think I could fulfill the assignment without the help of heaven. He asked if I would like a blessing. I've forgotten how it was arranged that I would see Elder Alvin R. Dyer, but that was especially pleasant for me, since I had been a priest once in a ward where he was the bishop, the president of my quorum. He listened sympathetically to my story, put his hands on my head, and gave me a blessing that included words like this as a promise: "In this assignment, and in many others which will come to you, your mind will be guided in channels toward the truth." That blessing gave me confidence, maybe too much confidence. The committee began its work. And after months of what seemed to me futile effort, I felt some desperation, much as you do when heaven seems to withhold its help in a task you know matters and is beyond you.

I somehow managed to arrange another interview. This one was with President Harold B. Lee. He received me in a kindly way. In my anxiety, I soon blurted out my question: "President Lee, how do I get revelation?"

He smiled. I am glad he didn't laugh, since it was an odd question to ask. But he answered my question with a story. It was essentially this. He said that during World War II he had been part of a group studying the question "What should the Church be doing for its members in the military service?" He said they conducted interviews at bases up and down the country. They had data gathered. They had the data analyzed. They went back for more interviews. But still, no plan emerged.

Then he gave me the lesson, which I now give to you, in about these words: "Hal, when we had done all we knew how to do, when we had our backs to the wall, then God gave us the revelation. Hal, if you want to get revelation, do your homework."

I suppose I should have been embarrassed to take his time to learn what the Lord told us all long ago. You recall the rebuke to Oliver Cowdery and to you and me and to all of our Father's children who are called to duties that take the powers of heaven. You remember the words. I am always impressed at how kindly they really were:

> Be patient, my son, for it is wisdom in me, and it is not expedient that you should translate at this present time.
>
> Behold, the work which you are called to do is to write for my servant Joseph.
>
> And, behold, it is because that you did not continue as you commenced, when you began to translate, that I have taken away this privilege from you.
>
> Do not murmur, my son, for it is wisdom in me that I have dealt with you after this manner.
>
> Behold, you have not understood; you have supposed that I would give it unto you, when you took no thought save it was to ask me.
>
> But, behold, I say unto you, that you must study it out in your mind; then you must ask me if it be right, and if it is right I will cause that your bosom shall burn within you; therefore, you shall feel that it is right.
>
> But if it be not right you shall have no such feelings, but you shall have a stupor of thought that shall cause you to forget the thing which is wrong; therefore, you cannot write that which is sacred save it be given you from me.

Now, if you had known this you could have translated; nevertheless, it is not expedient that you should translate now. (D&C 9:3–10.)

Now, in fairness to Oliver Cowdery, he had some reason to be confused. The Prophet Joseph seemed to have the windows of heaven opened to him. The words of revelation came to him, both to translate the Book of Mormon and to give us the revelations in the Doctrine and Covenants, at a speed that could easily have misled Oliver.

I bear you my solemn testimony that the Lord opens the heavens to his servants today. He will answer your prayers for help beyond your human understanding. But I also bear you my testimony that the words "study it out" mean a degree of patience, labor, and persistence commensurate with the value of what you seek.

Alma gave his son advice that is good for us. He said: "Preach unto them repentance, and faith on the Lord Jesus Christ; teach them to humble themselves and to be meek and lowly in heart; teach them to withstand every temptation of the devil, with their faith on the Lord Jesus Christ. Teach them to never be weary of good works, but to be meek and lowly in heart; for such shall find rest to their souls." (Alma 37:33–34.)

The good works that really matter require the help of heaven. And the help of heaven requires working past the point of fatigue so far that only the meek and lowly will keep going long enough. The Lord doesn't put us through this test just to give us a grade; he does it because the process will change us.

President Harold B. Lee described that once in general conference. He said: "To become converted, according to the scriptures, meant having a change of heart and the moral character of a person turned from the controlled power of sin into a righteous life. It meant to 'wait patiently on the Lord' until one's prayers can be answered." (*Conference Report*, April 1971, p. 92.)

If we are going to do our duty, we are going to need the powers of heaven. And if we are going to be given access to the powers of heaven, we are going to have to learn to wait upon the Lord.

The word *wait* in scriptural language means to hope for or anticipate. Surely the great prophet Isaiah meant that, and I think he meant more, when he made us a glorious promise. It's a promise I carved for my oldest son, Henry, when he had just turned twelve. I carved it on a board. The idea was that we would put the board on a wall for my son, and when certain things happened in his life, we would carve a record of that event. I carved the board first after he turned thirteen. He had already received his Eagle badge, so the word *deacon* is not carved there. It begins with *teacher*. The plaque goes through *teacher, priest, elder, mission,* and *marriage.* When we started, it was empty. So I knew it needed something nice at the top; it needed a crest and a motto. Since he had just won his Eagle Scout badge, I carved an eagle at the top with a legend suggested by Isaiah—"On Eagles' Wings"—as his motto.

I wish there had been more room on the board so that I could have carved there the whole lesson. How would he be lifted as on eagles' wings? "They that wait upon the Lord shall renew their strength; they shall mount up with wings as eagles; they shall run, and not be weary; and they shall walk, and not faint." (Isaiah 40:31.)

If I were to try to help you, or my son, have that glorious blessing—that you not be weary in doing your duty—I would tell you the little I know about waiting upon the Lord.

The scriptures, what I see around me, and my own

experience tell me that this scripture has a key in it: "And now I would that ye should be humble, and be submissive and gentle; easy to be entreated; full of patience and long-suffering; being temperate in all things; being diligent in keeping the commandments of God at all times; asking for whatsoever things ye stand in need, both spiritual and temporal; always returning thanks unto God for whatsoever things ye do receive. And see that ye have faith, hope, and charity, and then ye will always abound in good works. And may the Lord bless you, and keep your garments spotless." (Alma 7:23–25.)

Being submissive, gentle, easy to be entreated, and patient are all attributes. But the actions Alma commends to us are to ask for what we need and to return thanks. Please don't think of that as a routine command to say your prayers. Oh, it is much more than that. If you pray, if you talk to God, if you plead for the help you need, and if you thank him not only for help but for the patience and gentleness that come from not receiving all you desire right away—or perhaps ever—I promise you that you will draw closer to him. And then you will become diligent and long-suffering.

Let me tell you another way you can bring down on you the powers of heaven. Just as you sometimes feel the great need to have heaven's help in your service, you must often sense a need for help to resist evil. Just as prayer is a simple choice, there is another simple choice you can make that you might live clean in a wicked world.

In an earlier chapter I quoted President George Albert Smith's statement that "there is a division line well defined that separates the Lord's territory from Lucifer's." You can decide to move toward the Savior and to live on his side of the line. Every person is faced with different alternatives, but the choice is always clear. You remember that Mormon told his son, Moroni, exactly what marks the line and why it is so clear. Think about this when you decide what video you might watch, what magazine you might pick up, or whatever you might do. Mormon said: "For behold, the Spirit of Christ is given to every man, that he may know good from evil; wherefore, I show unto you the way to judge; for every thing which inviteth to do good, and to persuade to believe in Christ, is sent forth by the power and gift of Christ; wherefore ye may know with a perfect knowledge it is of God. But whatsoever thing persuadeth men to do evil, and believe not in Christ, and deny him, and serve not God, then ye may know with a perfect knowledge it is of the devil; for after this manner doth the devil work, for he persuadeth no man to do good, no, not one; neither do his angels; neither do they who subject themselves unto him." (Moroni 7:16–17.)

I plead with you to take that seriously. The world will become more wicked. You will need the help of heaven to keep the commandments. You will need it more and more as the days go on. Satan will expand the space that is not safe. He will try every way he can to persuade you that there is no danger in trying to come as close as you can to that dividing line. At the same time, he is trying to persuade people that there really is no line at all. Because he knows that you know it is there, he will say to you, "Come closer to the line."

But you can bring the protective powers of heaven down on you by simply deciding to go toward the Savior, to wait on him. Satan will tell you, as he has done regularly for ages, that you will not be happy in safety, that you must come near his ground to live the happy life. Well, that is a clear choice, too. Here it is, put about as plainly as you will get it, in the words of Nephi: "Wherefore, men are free according to the flesh; and all things are given them which are expedient unto man. And they are free to choose liberty and eternal life, through the great Mediator of all men, or to choose captivity and death, according to the captivity and power of the devil; for he seeketh that all men might be miserable like unto himself." (2 Nephi 2:27.)

I hope you will remember that when you see some beautifully packaged, cleverly advertised invitation to go into Satan's territory. It will be funny or pleasant or charming or glamorous; but remember, he wants you to be as miserable as he is himself.

As long as we are being plain about choices, there is another way you can decide to wait upon the Lord. Again, it is a choice to move to safety by doing your duty. It takes a decision about how to use your time and about where to put your ego. And you can use it in the next week. Here it is again from that plain speaker, President Harold B. Lee:

> Now the only safety we have as members of this church is to do exactly what the Lord said to the Church in that day when the Church was organized. We must learn to give heed to the words and commandments that the Lord shall give through his prophet, "as he receiveth them, walking in all holiness before me; . . . as if from mine own mouth, in all patience and faith" (D&C 21:4–5). There will be some things that take patience and faith. You may not like what comes from the authority of the Church. It may contradict your political views. . . . It may interfere with some of your social life. But if you listen to these things, as if from the mouth of the Lord himself, with patience and faith, the promise is that "the gates of hell shall not prevail against you; yea, and the Lord God will disperse the powers of darkness from before you, and cause the heavens to shake for your good, and his name's glory" (D&C 21:6). (*Conference Report,* October 1970, p. 152.)

I'll add a promise to you of my own. If you will wait

99

upon the Lord the next time you listen to the General Authorities of the Church, if you will forget about them as human personalities and listen for the Lord's voice, I promise you that you will recognize it in the words spoken by his servants. You will have a quiet assurance that those human beings are called of God and that God honors their calls.

I will make you that same promise about the next time your bishop speaks to you. I was in my ward not long ago, and our bishop spoke. As my wife and I left, we said to each other, "You could feel, couldn't you, when the Holy Ghost came?" He bore testimony, and I knew that my bishop, who is my neighbor, was called of God as surely as any human being has ever been.

Try it with your bishop. He might decide to talk to you sometime soon. Listen. Wait upon the Lord as he speaks. Don't worry about him as a human being; just listen and see if you can hear the voice of the Lord. I promise you not only that you will hear what you should hear, but that you will see that his call is a call from God, and you will find it far easier to be a faithful servant in your ward.

You might even try it with your home teachers or your visiting teachers. While they are in your home, wait upon the Lord. Listen and see if you can know what it is God would have you do. It may not even be in their words. It may be things that will come to you while they speak, but you will know. And you will know that it is coming to you because you are waiting upon the Lord by honoring his servants. And when you see that God can honor the callings of such humble people, you will find your faith increased that he may magnify what you are doing in your own service. You won't always see the miracles that come from your work, which is probably a blessing. If you did, you would get proud. But you can often underestimate what God is doing as he honors your calling.

I want to tell you a story about waiting on the Lord. My father once told it to me with the intention of chuckling at himself. It's a story about his trying to do his duty, just the way you try to do your duty.

Now, you have to know a little bit about my father. His name was Henry Eyring, like mine. His work in chemistry was substantial enough to bring him many honors, but he was still a member of a ward of the Church with his duty to do. To appreciate this story, you have to realize that it occurred when he was nearly eighty and had bone cancer. He had bone cancer so badly in his hips that he could hardly move. The pain was great.

Dad was the senior high councilor in his stake, and he had the responsibility for the welfare farm. An assignment was given to weed a field of onions, so Dad assigned himself to go work on the farm. He never told me how hard it was, but I have met several people who were with him that day. I talked to one of them on the phone, and he said that he was weeding in the row next to Dad through much of the day. He told me the same thing that others who were there that day have told me. He said that the pain was so great that Dad was pulling himself along on his stomach with his elbows. He couldn't kneel. The pain was too great for him to kneel. Everyone who has talked to me about that day has remarked how Dad smiled and laughed and talked happily with them as they worked in that field of onions.

Now, this is the joke Dad told me on himself afterward. He said he was there at the end of the day. After all the work was finished and the onions were all weeded, someone said to him, "Henry, good heavens! You didn't pull those weeds, did you? Those weeds were sprayed two days ago, and they were going to die anyway."

101

Dad just roared. He thought that was the funniest thing. He thought it was a great joke on himself. He had worked through the day in the wrong weeds. They had been sprayed and would have died anyway.

When Dad told me this story, I knew how tough it was. So I asked him, "Dad, how could you make a joke out of that? How could you take it so pleasantly?" He said something to me that I will never forget, and I hope you won't. He said, "Hal, I wasn't there for the weeds."

Now, you'll be in an onion patch much of your life. So will I. It will be hard to see the powers of heaven magnifying us or our efforts. It may even be hard to see our work being of any value at all. And sometimes our work won't go well.

But you didn't come for the weeds. You came for the Savior. And if you pray, and if you choose to be clean, and if you choose to follow God's servants, you will be able to work and wait long enough to bring down the powers of heaven.

I was with Dad in the White House in Washington, D.C., the morning he got the National Medal of Science from the president of the United States. I missed the days when he got all the other medals and prizes. But, oh, how I'd like to be with him on the morning he gets the prize he won for his days in the onion patches. He was there to wait on the Lord. And you and I can do that, too.

I pray that we will. Then maybe we can hear this said of us: "And now, my son, I trust that I shall have great joy in you, because of your steadiness and your faithfulness unto God; for as you have commenced in your youth to look to the Lord your God, even so I hope that you will continue in keeping his commandments; for blessed is he that endureth to the end." (Alma 38:2.)

The next time I get asked by my bishop or my quorum

leader to do something, here is what I am going to try to remember: "Behold, I say unto you that ye must pray always, and not faint; that ye must not perform any thing unto the Lord save in the first place ye shall pray unto the Father in the name of Christ, that he will consecrate thy performance unto thee, that thy performance may be for the welfare of thy soul." (2 Nephi 32:9.) And while I'm working at it, my plan is to remember that I'm doing it for the Lord.

I promise you that if you will be patient and diligent, you will have the blessing of knowing that you are doing what the Lord would have you do. And you will remember that while you're in that onion patch, you are not there for the weeds. (That will be important sometimes when the weeds don't come out easily.) You will feel the approval of God.

"But they that wait upon the Lord shall renew their strength; they shall mount up with wings as eagles; they shall run, and not be weary; and they shall walk, and not faint." (Isaiah 40:31.)

Dad never got better. He just got worse. So you might say, "Well, he waited upon the Lord, but he couldn't run and he couldn't walk." But that was true only in this life. There will be a day for you and me when, whatever difficulties and limitations we have here, we will have that promise fulfilled for us. We will be lifted up as on eagles' wings if we have waited upon the Lord.

CHAPTER 9

SURRENDER TO CHRIST

Have you thought very much about that great, mighty change that the scriptures talk about? Alma the Younger described it this way: "The Lord said unto me: Marvel not that all mankind, yea, men and women, all nations, kindreds, tongues and people, must be born again; yea, born of God, changed from their carnal and fallen state, to a state of righteousness, being redeemed of God, becoming his sons and daughters; and thus they become new creatures; and unless they do this, they can in nowise inherit the kingdom of God." (Mosiah 27:25–26.)

Have you ever thought, "Wouldn't it be nice to have that experience?" Well, the scriptures don't suggest that it would be nice; they say that it's *necessary* in order for you and me to have what it is we want, which is eternal life. Now, so that you don't get too discouraged, consider what President Ezra Taft Benson said: "When we have undergone this mighty change, which is brought about only through faith in Jesus Christ and through the operation of the Spirit

---

From a talk given at a Ricks College Devotional, 21 September 1993.

upon us, it is as though we have become a new person. Thus, the change is likened to a new birth. Thousands of you have experienced this change. You have forsaken lives of sin, sometimes deep and offensive sin, and through applying the blood of Christ in your lives have become clean. You have no more disposition to return to your old ways. You are in reality a new person. This is what is meant by a change of heart." ("A Mighty Change of Heart," *Ensign,* October 1989, p. 4.)

I want you to know that what we're talking about is real. This is not just "Wouldn't it be nice?" but something that can be done. Let me tell you how. The key is found in one word, and the word is *surrender.* Now, some people are used to being tough and strong, and they feel that surrendering is not something you should do very often. But we're not talking about surrendering to a human being. President David O. McKay said that "human nature *can* be changed, here and now." He then quoted this statement from Beverly Nichols: "You do change human nature, your own human nature, if you surrender it to Christ. Human nature has been changed in the past. Human nature must be changed on an enormous scale in the future, unless the world is to be drowned in its own blood. And only Christ can change it." (David O. McKay, *Stepping Stones to an Abundant Life* [Salt Lake City: Deseret Book Co., 1971], p. 23; as quoted in Ezra Taft Benson, "Born of God," *Ensign,* July 1989, p. 4.)

I've talked with good people who have considered themselves "born-again Christians," and I've realized that they have had profound experiences through their love for the Savior. They have seen a need to change, have made changes in their lives, and have "accepted Christ," as they refer to it. What I want to teach you is that the kind of surrender we're speaking of is not a simple declaration, nor is it a single experience. President Marion G. Romney described it as something far deeper and more specific than a single great moment in our lives: "Everyone who would know God the Eternal Father and Jesus Christ, whom he has sent, must receive such knowledge by the Spirit. Church members have, of course, been through the process. They have been baptized and confirmed members of the Church and have had hands laid upon their heads for the gift of the Holy Ghost. Through these ordinances the door is unlocked. Submission to this is absolutely essential to rebirth." ("'Except a Man Be Born Again,'" *Ensign*, November 1981, p. 15.)

Do you know what it really means to be submissive to the ordinances of the gospel? It means much more than agreeing to let someone baptize you. The ordinances are the key to the "mighty change" spoken of in the scriptures. There may be some who feel that they've experienced a true spiritual rebirth without receiving those ordinances by proper authority, but they haven't. When I was a boy, someone who held the priesthood laid his hands on my head and told me that I had the right to the companionship of the Holy Ghost. I testify to you that had that ordinance not been performed, I wouldn't have that right today. But for me to be *submissive* to that ordinance is another matter. To be submissive I must recognize my need for the gift of the Holy Ghost, I must plead for it with all my heart, and I must live worthy of it.

And the Holy Ghost will come, not because of one great moment, but because of many little moments of submission. President Benson explained that "part of this mighty change of heart is to feel godly sorrow for our sins. This is what is meant by a broken heart and a contrite spirit. . . . God's gifts are sufficient to help us overcome every sin and weakness if we will but turn to Him for help.

. . . Most repentance does not involve sensational or dramatic changes, but rather is a step-by-step, steady, and consistent movement toward godliness." ("A Mighty Change
of Heart," p. 5.)

It is a step-by-step process. You don't submit once; you
submit over and over again. And one of the ways to submit
is to try to do what you can to have the Holy Ghost with
you as your companion. For instance, you can pray and ask
Heavenly Father if there's anything he would have you do.
You might ask, "What would the Savior do if he were here?
Is there anybody he might wish he could visit?" If you'll ask
questions like that, the Holy Ghost will come and you'll
feel nudges about things you can do for other people. When
you go and do those things, you're on the Lord's errand, and
when you're on the Lord's errand, you qualify for the gift of
the Holy Ghost. And when the Holy Ghost is with you, he
has a purifying effect that changes your nature.

President Romney described how we can know when
that change is occurring: "While conversion may be accom-
plished in stages, one is not really converted in the full
sense of the term unless and until he is at heart a new person. *Born again* is the scriptural term.

"In one who is wholly converted, desire for things inim-
ical to the gospel of Jesus Christ has actually died, and sub-
stituted therefor is a love of God with a fixed and
controlling determination to keep his commandments."
(*Look to God and Live* [Salt Lake City: Deseret Book Co.,
1973], p. 109.)

I've known a few prophets. You'll hear them criticized
and attacked, and people will sometimes talk about their
failures or their weaknesses, because they're not perfect. But
I'll tell you this: Each time I'm with any of those whom you
sustain as prophets, seers, and revelators, I'm struck with
how the atonement of Jesus Christ has worked in their

lives. There is a kindness, a desire to give their all and to do what the Lord would want, to bless and help and care about people that is beyond what they could have done by just wanting to change or resolving to change. The Atonement is real, it works in people's lives, and you don't have to be an Apostle or a prophet to have it work. If you will begin to do the things he would have you do, you really will find that your desire to do evil will decrease. I testify that you don't need to be afraid or discouraged. The Atonement is real. As you steadily do the things the Lord would have you do, a change will occur in you, and Satan's ability to lead you into the things that will destroy you and bring misery to you will become lessened.

Now, the key in all of this is to have a soft heart. A soft heart has nothing to do with being a coward. In fact, the bravest people I've ever known have had the softest hearts. I've known of situations in which the Lord's servants have put their lives in jeopardy because of their love for God and his children. When people love enough, and their hearts are softened enough, there's nothing they wouldn't do in the service of the Lord Jesus Christ. A Latter-day Saint with a soft heart is courageous, strong, and able to do far more than those who think of themselves as tough. This is what the Savior said about a soft heart: "And ye shall offer for a sacrifice unto me a broken heart and a contrite spirit. And whoso cometh unto me with a broken heart and a contrite spirit, him will I baptize with fire and with the Holy Ghost. . . . Behold, I have come unto the world to bring redemption unto the world, to save the world from sin. Therefore, whoso repenteth and cometh unto me as a little child, him will I receive, for of such is the kingdom of God. Behold, for such I have laid down my life, and have taken it up again; therefore repent, and come unto me ye ends of the earth, and be saved." (3 Nephi 9:20–22.)

What are some things you could do to have a soft heart? First of all, don't think of repentance as something you do after you've made a very serious mistake. Think of repentance as what you do every day. Find a moment each day to review in your mind those things that might have disappointed your Heavenly Father and your Savior, and then go and humbly plead for forgiveness. I would suggest that you do that especially on Sundays when you take the sacrament. Submit yourself to the sacramental ordinance. Don't simply be there, but say to yourself, "I really want to renew my covenants, and I need to have the Lord's forgiveness." Plead with him for his forgiveness. If you'll do that, you'll find that sacrament meetings will take on a greater meaning to you than you've known in the past. You'll come away refreshed and strengthened.

Another way to obtain a soft heart is to make sure you don't focus too much on yourself or your personal problems and struggles. Instead of thinking of yourself primarily as someone who is seeking purification, think of yourself as someone who is trying to find out who around you needs your help. Pray that way and then reach out. When you act under such inspiration, it will have a sanctifying effect on you.

Now, if you'll do these things, something wonderful will happen. The Lord will try you, but if you'll work a little bit and show him that you're willing to try, he will bless you and give you more strength and understanding. "He that will not harden his heart, to him is given the greater portion of the word, until it is given unto him to know the mysteries of God until he know them in full." (Alma 12:10.) I testify that if you'll just try, you'll find an increasing capacity to know spiritual things and to feel spiritual things. And as the Atonement works in your life, you'll feel less inclination to do that which is evil. The ordinances you've received are real. God honors them, and if you'll just honor them by being submissive to the covenants you have made, the Holy Ghost will be poured out upon you and you'll see better who God is, who you are, and how you can help change the world for the better. Your surrender will have led to a victory.

CHAPTER 10

GOING HOME

I want to discuss the idea of going home. All of us know that happiness in some way centers on a family—both in this world and in the next.

Only as I've grown older have I come to understand what my parents did for me. Of all the influences they had on me, perhaps the most powerful was the desire to somehow be worthy to go home again to my Heavenly Father and live with him forever. And by their example, and a little preaching, they taught me how I can find my way back to my Heavenly Father. Since I learned this by using scripture to understand experience, I'll share it with you that way. But let me first tell you the lesson so it won't take you so long to recognize it. It's this simple chain:

1. We will find our way home to our Heavenly Father only if we win the companionship of the Holy Ghost so we can recognize truth.

2. The companionship of the Holy Ghost requires our being clean.

From a talk given at a BYU Devotional, 18 November 1986.

3. Being clean requires exercising faith in the Lord Jesus Christ unto repentance.

That sounds so simple, but it is so hard because there is a Satan, the father of lies, who also knows that simple chain which will give us the companionship of the Spirit of Truth. His determination to keep you and me from following this chain explains the blunt language Brigham Young used to describe our challenge: "The men and women who desire to obtain seats in the celestial kingdom will find that they must battle every day." (*Discourses of Brigham Young*, comp. John A. Widtsoe [Salt Lake City: Deseret Book Co., 1954], p. 392.)

The nature of that battle, and its difficulty, came clear to me in an airplane not long ago. It was a long flight, so I wrote and read and thought. As I'd rushed out the door from home, I'd taken one of my son's worn and inexpensive editions of the Book of Mormon. As I read it on the plane, I saw that his seminary teacher had led him through it. I began to move through the book to see what passages were marked and annotated in red ink, wondering what that teacher had taught him was important. I went along and then my eyes fell on these words of the prophet Nephi: "Wherefore, if ye have sought to do wickedly in the days of your probation, then ye are found unclean before the judgment-seat of God; and no unclean thing can dwell with God; wherefore, ye must be cast off forever." (1 Nephi 10:21.)

Those words made my heart burn, and my eyes too. I thought for a minute of what our Heavenly Father might feel as he had to send children he loved away, forever, because they could not be with him.

A few minutes later, after having lunch and visiting with the person next to me, I picked up a national news magazine from the pocket in the seat in front of me and began to leaf through it. I came to the movie reviews. Only three films were reviewed. All three were reported to portray real people committing acts of immorality, some fortunately beyond my powers of imagination. The reviewers warned me about only one of them, on the grounds that it would be boring, and urged me to see the other two.

Just minutes later I moved a few chapters through the book of 1 Nephi, where these words seemed to appear in bold print: "Behold, I say unto you, the kingdom of God is not filthy, and there cannot any unclean thing enter into the kingdom of God; wherefore there must needs be a place of filthiness prepared for that which is filthy." (1 Nephi 15:34.)

That set me to pondering. I thought of you and of me. We have a problem. We live in a world where there are voices competing for our belief. They claim the authority of truth. Some are clearly lying and some are not. And you and I need to know what is true and what is not, out of far more than curiosity. We need to know. And we need to be sure.

Some of those voices—some of the loudest—tell you that the questions which matter will yield to reason. And they even warn you that those who purport to answer questions without using their rules of rational analysis are to be distrusted and even despised.

Your common sense and experience tell you something else. So does mine. Let me illustrate for you what I know about the questions that matter and how they are answered by telling you about the last conversations I had with my father.

He was suffering through the end of a long struggle with bone cancer. He still weighed enough and was in such pain that it was hard work to move him from a chair to his bed. Others far more heroic than I spent the months and the days caring for him. But I took some turns on the midnight-to-dawn shift.

The effects of disease had removed the powers of reason he'd used to make a mark that is still visible in science. He seemed to me almost like a child as we talked through the night. Most of his memories were of riding across the range together with his father in Old Mexico. But sometimes even those happy pictures could not crowd from his mind the terrible pain.

One night when I was not with him and the pain seemed more than he could bear, he somehow got out of bed and on his knees beside it—I know not how. He pled with God to know why he was suffering so. And the next morning he said, with quiet firmness, "I know why now. God needs brave sons."

Now, when someone tells you the questions that matter yield only to some rational analysis, remember that the stunning achievements of reason over the past three hundred years have sprung from what is called the "scientific method." I hope you'll also remember, as I always will, the scientist Henry Eyring on his knees, when the questions that really mattered yielded to the method for finding truth he'd learned as a little boy at his mother's knee in Old Mexico. This was long before he took the train to Tucson, and Berkeley, and Madison, and then on to Berlin and Princeton to use the scientific method to create theories that changed the scientific world. What he learned on his knees brought him peace and changed my life.

It changed my life, but reading this story today will change yours only if you know that the answer to his prayer was true. And you can know that only the way he did and the way I do—by the gentle voice of the Holy Ghost speaking to your heart.

God has blessed us with sure guides to truth. Some of us

have been blessed with parents who knew where to find truth. All of us can listen to the voice of a living prophet to whom God speaks the truth and asked that he tell us. The words of the prophet, and the words of scripture, are the rod which Lehi saw would lead us to the tree of life.

But many have heard those words, and read them, and still have not known that they are true. The method of knowing truth requires that both he who speaks and he who hears be guided by the Holy Ghost. You and I can only know it is the truth if we can hear the Holy Spirit confirm and expand it in our own hearts. Of all the methods of searching for the truth, that is the one you and I need most.

The key is in the words of Nephi I was reading on the plane that day. It might surprise you that in a passage on being clean would be the key to gaining the Holy Ghost as your constant companion. It shouldn't surprise you, though, because in all but a few references to the Holy Spirit in the scriptures, the cry to be clean is close by. The pairing of spiritual cleanliness and the gifts of the Spirit, the power to know and speak truth, becomes plain in the words of Nephi.

Nephi wanted to know for himself that what his father said he had seen in a vision was true. His father had reported seeing the fearsome landscape we move across in life, either toward eternal life or toward forever being shut out from our Father. Nephi knew he had to know for himself. This is how he pursued the truth:

> And it came to pass after I, Nephi, having heard all the words of my father, concerning the things which he saw in a vision, and also the things which he spake by the power of the Holy Ghost, which power he received by faith on the Son of God—and the Son of God was the Messiah who should come—I, Nephi, was desirous also that I might see, and hear, and know of these things, by the power of the Holy

Ghost, which is the gift of God unto all those who diligently seek him, as well in times of old as in the time that he should manifest himself unto the children of men. For he is the same yesterday, to-day, and forever; and the way is prepared for all men from the foundation of the world, if it so be that they repent and come unto him. (1 Nephi 10:17–18.)

Now you can see why President Ezra Taft Benson, a modern prophet of God, repeatedly taught us to read the Book of Mormon. The Book of Mormon is the most powerful written testimony we have that Jesus is the Christ. What did Nephi say was the basis for receiving the Holy Ghost? Faith in the Lord Jesus Christ. Will reading the Book of Mormon now and then ensure faith in the Lord Jesus Christ? You wouldn't count on it if you read Nephi carefully. He said the Holy Ghost is "the gift of God unto all those who diligently seek him." Diligently surely means regularly. And it surely means pondering and praying. And the praying will surely include a fervent pleading to know the truth. Anything less would hardly be diligent. And anything less will not be enough for you and for me.

That diligence will allow faith to grow, and then will come a desire to repent and a confidence that forgiveness is possible. Real repentance requires as diligent a pursuit as real faith. The forgiveness we seek is possible only through the ordinance of baptism, performed by God's authorized servants, and by our then keeping the covenants we make with God.

If you are not yet a member of the Church, you are required to seek baptism by those who hold the priesthood of God. If you have been baptized, it means diligently keeping the covenants.

Each week you and I can hear in the sacramental prayer the promise we so much need to see fulfilled: "And always remember him and keep his commandments which he has given them; that they may always have his Spirit to be with them." (D&C 20:77.)

That might well raise a question in your mind. You may now be reading the Book of Mormon diligently, daily. You may be praying often and with real intent. That may have led to such faith in Jesus Christ that you remember him with love. And that surely will have both led you to a broken heart and to seeking forgiveness for past sins and a determination to keep every commandment. But you may still say, "With all that, I don't seem to get the promptings of what is true as easily as I think I should if I really have his Spirit, the Holy Ghost, to be with me."

The Prophet Joseph Smith once faced a test of patience beyond what most of us have endured. He was locked in Liberty Jail, and the Saints were suffering. He pled in prayer for immediate action. God granted him, in answer to his prayer, something more than he asked for. He told him how he would pour out knowledge from heaven upon the heads of the Saints. He talked about the priceless knowledge of knowing how to act so that the Saints could be servants of God, worthy of his power. And then he told him, and he told you and me, how it will feel as knowledge of the truth comes. Here it is, at the end of section 121 of the Doctrine and Covenants: "Let thy bowels also be full of charity towards all men, and to the household of faith, and let virtue garnish thy thoughts unceasingly; then shall thy confidence wax strong in the presence of God; and the doctrine of the priesthood shall distil upon thy soul as the dews from heaven. The Holy Ghost shall be thy constant companion, and thy scepter an unchanging scepter of righteousness and truth; and thy dominion shall be an everlasting dominion, and without compulsory means it shall flow unto thee forever and ever." (D&C 121:45–46.)

You and I need to be patient, and for a reason. A quick

reading of the Book of Mormon, a few prayers, a shallow attempt at repentance, a casual regard for the covenants we've made—of course, that is not enough. The scriptures use over and over again the word "steadiness" to describe faithful disciples of the Lord Jesus Christ. When faith and repentance and diligent efforts to live the commandments have gone on long enough that virtue garnishes our thoughts unceasingly, then the doctrine of the priesthood, the truthful answers to the questions that really matter, will distill upon us as the dews from heaven.

That's been my experience with seeking the confirmation of truth by the Spirit of God. I have at times sought it by singular effort, in times of great need, and it has come. Investigators have that experience when they reach the point where they must know if the Book of Mormon is true.

But far more often for me, I notice the Spirit's presence in quiet confirmations at times when all I seem to have done is plod on in diligence, doing the simple things—searching the scriptures with a prayer in my heart and with more concern for others, and therefore less time for pursuits that let Satan, the father of lies, entice me. It's in periods of that steadiness that I notice the Holy Ghost, almost in the way you're surprised to discover that your shoes are wet from the dew formed on the grass overnight, and I look up and realize that my mind has been enlightened and my heart has been enlarged.

Perhaps the most difficult part of the whole process is not to keep going but to begin. That's true with many projects we face, but this most important project involves an added difficulty. It is that you have a skilled adversary who both lies and urges you to lie.

Of all his falsehoods, perhaps none is so commonly used and so frequently successful as this: "No one knows, so wait to repent."

It's not true. First of all, you know. That almost invariably means that the price you must pay to procrastinate repentance is to lie. For instance, you may take the sacrament when you know you are unworthy. You may be perfectly content to accept that deception on top of the effects of the sin itself, but you pay a price. Even a man who looked with the eyes of science could see that pain. Lewis Thomas seemed almost surprised when he wrote the following about lie detectors and their implications:

> As I understand it, a human being cannot tell a lie, even a small one, without setting off a kind of smoke alarm somewhere deep in a dark lobule of the brain, resulting in the sudden discharge of nerve impulses, or the sudden outpouring of neurohormones of some sort, or both. The outcome, recorded by the lie-detector gadgetry, is a highly reproducible cascade of changes in the electrical conductivity of the skin, the heart rate, and the manner of breathing, similar to the responses to various kinds of stress.
>
> Lying, then, is stressful, even when we do it for protection, or relief, or escape, or profit, or just for the pure pleasure of lying and getting away with it. It is a strain, distressing enough to cause the emission of signals to and from the central nervous system warning that something has gone wrong. It is, in a pure physiological sense, an unnatural act. (Lewis Thomas, *Late Night Thoughts on Listening to Mahler's Ninth Symphony* [New York: Bantam Books, 1984], p. 128.)

It is unnatural in far more than a physiological sense. It is contrary to the nature of our spirits. You are a spirit child of God, a God of truth. Whatever stress your body feels from your choosing to lie, your spirit must be torn far more. The relief of that load that comes from confessing and moving forward to full repentance will more than compensate for whatever unpleasant consequences honesty brings upon you.

121

Perhaps even more important than recognizing that you know what you have done is knowing that God knows. You and I can't be fooled into believing anything is hidden. The Savior taught us in 2 Nephi: "Wo unto them that seek deep to hide their counsel from the Lord! And their works are in the dark; and they say: Who seeth us, and who knoweth us? . . . Behold, I will show unto them, saith the Lord of Hosts, that I know all their works. For shall the work say of him that made it, he made me not? Or shall the thing framed say of him that framed it, he had no understanding?" (2 Nephi 27:27.)

And not only does our Heavenly Father see all we do, but he sees us with such eyes of love that Enoch, who saw God's reaction to sin in the time of Noah in vision, asked of God in surprise, "How is it that thou canst weep, seeing thou art holy, and from all eternity to all eternity?" (Moses 7:29.)

Explaining that he saw the terrible, inescapable consequences of unrepented and unforgiven sins, God said to Enoch: "And the whole heavens shall weep over them, even all the workmanship of mine hands; wherefore should not the heavens weep, seeing these shall suffer?" (Moses 7:37.)

God knows all we have done. And while he cannot look on sin with the least degree of allowance, he looks on us with compassion beyond our capacity to measure. When the scripture speaks of the whole heavens weeping, I think of another picture, given to us by the Prophet Joseph Smith. This is what he said: "The spirits of the just are . . . blessed in their departure to the world of spirits. Enveloped in flaming fire, they are not far from us, and know and understand our thoughts, feelings, and motions, and are often pained therewith." (*History of the Church of Jesus*

Christ of Latter-day Saints, ed. B. H. Roberts, 2d ed. rev., 7 vols. [Salt Lake City: Deseret Book Co., 1974], 6:52.)

These words pain me when I think of those I have loved and who loved me who are surely now among the spirits of the just. The realization that they feel pain for us and that the God of Heaven weeps because of our unrepented sin is surely enough to soften our hearts and move us to action. And it is surely reason enough to avoid even the approaches, the very thought, of committing serious sin.

If you could form one picture in your mind today, let it be of a son, Nephi. His father told him of his vision about how to get back home again to Heavenly Father and to the Savior. But for Nephi it wasn't enough to hear his father's words. He had to know the truth for himself, to be sure he would know the way. Nephi taught about the loving God who has provided a way for us to come home:

> For he is the same yesterday, to-day, and forever; and the way is prepared for all men from the foundation of the world, if it so be that they repent and come unto him.
>
> For he that diligently seeketh shall find; and the mysteries of God shall be unfolded unto them, by the power of the Holy Ghost, as well in these times as in times of old, and as well in times of old as in times to come; wherefore, the course of the Lord is one eternal round.
>
> Therefore remember, O man, for all thy doings thou shalt be brought into judgment.
>
> Wherefore, if ye have sought to do wickedly in the days of your probation, then ye are found unclean before the judgment-seat of God; and no unclean thing can dwell with God; wherefore, ye must be cast off forever.
>
> And the Holy Ghost giveth authority that I should speak these things, and deny them not. (1 Nephi 10:18–22.)

Could I now give you two practical suggestions? First of all, the Holy Ghost is and must be very sensitive. He can be easily offended. Let me pass along a little advice the Prophet Joseph Smith gave to the leaders of the Church:

> Here is [an] important item. If you assemble from time to time, and proceed to discuss important questions, and pass decisions upon the same, and fail to note them down, by and by you will be driven to straits from which you will not be able to extricate yourselves, because you may be in a situation not to bring your faith to bear with sufficient perfection or power to obtain the desired information; or, perhaps, for neglecting to write these things when God had revealed them, not esteeming them of sufficient worth, the Spirit may withdraw, and God may be angry; and there is, or was, a vast knowledge, of infinite importance, which is now lost. (*Teachings of the Prophet Joseph Smith*, p. 73.)

I think that means that in your heart, at least, the attitude of writing down even the simplest things that may come from the Spirit would invite the Spirit back again.

One other bit of advice. Of all the times I have felt the promptings of the Spirit, they have come most forcefully and most surely when I was asking Heavenly Father what he would have me do for someone whom I loved and who I knew had a need.

When the prophet Mormon was putting together what we now find in the Book of Mormon, and he didn't know why he was told to put in certain things and not to put in others, he wrote: "I do this for a wise purpose; for thus it whispereth me, according to the workings of the Spirit of the Lord which is in me. And now I do not know all things; but the Lord knoweth all things which are to come; wherefore, he worketh in me to do according to his will." (Words of Mormon 1:7.)

And then, in the very next verse, it's almost as if Mormon is telling us why God is able to take him like a little child and lead him to do things without explaining the reasons for them: "And my prayer to God is concerning my brethren, that they may once again come to the knowledge of God, yea, the redemption of Christ; that they may once again be a delightsome people." (Words of Mormon 1:8.)

Years ago a wise father got a letter from a son in the mission field who wrote, "I can't get the feeling for this work. I'm discouraged." The father wrote back what you would think would be too simple a suggestion. He wrote back and said, "Forget yourself and go to work." My prayer is that, in our desire to have the companionship of the Holy Spirit, we might forget ourselves and go to work—and that we might truly seek the good of our Father's children. If with all our hearts we try to take his children home again, we'll be there too.

I pray that we might live in such a way that we will have the companionship of the Holy Spirit, that we might all go home again.

PART 3

HELPING OTHERS DRAW CLOSER TO GOD

CHAPTER 11

THE SPARK OF
FAITH

I think of those whose hearts ache over promises yet unfulfilled. Tonight, or tomorrow, many of us will pray with real intent, and perhaps with tears, over someone whose happiness would bring us happiness, who has been promised all the blessings of peace that come with baptism and the gift of the Holy Ghost, and yet who counts the promises worthless. None of us is immune, because all of us have circles of love large enough to include such people. My heart is drawn especially to those asking the question we all have asked: "How can I be sure I have done all I can to help?"

More than sixty years ago, President J. Reuben Clark, Jr., of the First Presidency, gave this answer, which I carry copied on a card: "It is my hope and my belief that the Lord never permits the light of faith wholly to be extinguished in any human heart, however faint the light may glow. The Lord has provided that there shall still be there a spark which, with teaching, with the spirit of righteousness, with love, with tenderness, with example, with living the

From a talk given at General Conference, 5 October 1986.

Gospel, shall brighten and glow again, however darkened the mind may have been. And if we shall fail so to reach those among us of our own whose faith has dwindled low, we shall fail in one of the main things which the Lord expects at our hands." (*Conference Report,* October 1936, p. 114.)

That lovely metaphor—of a spark, a spark of faith—gives me confidence. President Clark pictured the spark nearly hidden, almost smothered by the ashes of transgression. It may be so small that the person can't feel its warmth. The heart may be hardened. Even the Holy Spirit may have been forced to withdraw. But the spark still lives, and glows, and may be fanned to flame.

President Clark also suggested what we can do. He did not suggest a single approach to reach all people. But he described what every effort that succeeds in fanning the spark will include.

Teaching is first. But what should we teach? Suppose time and opportunity are scarce, as they generally are with people who don't think they need your teaching. If you had the gift, and the chance, to teach only one thing, what would it be?

For me the answer is illustrated in the success of a great man whose heart ached over someone he loved. His name was Alma, and his son, Alma, went about trying to destroy the true Church. You remember that in response to the prayers of his father, and of faithful members of the Church, God sent an angel to rebuke the son.

The rebuke brought young Alma such remorse that he would have been destroyed had he not remembered his father's teaching. He described it this way: "And now, for three days and for three nights was I racked, even with the pains of a damned soul. And it came to pass that as I was thus racked with torment, while I was harrowed up by the

130

memory of my many sins, behold, I remembered also to have heard my father prophesy unto the people concerning the coming of one Jesus Christ, a Son of God, to atone for the sins of the world. Now, as my mind caught hold upon this thought, I cried within my heart: O Jesus, thou Son of God, have mercy on me, who am in the gall of bitterness, and am encircled about by the everlasting chains of death." (Alma 36:16–18.)

Because his father had taught him that the Savior was his only source of hope, Alma began the process which took him to full repentance. If I had the chance to teach one thing, it would be what it means and how it feels to exercise faith in Jesus Christ unto repentance.

To do it, I would try to take the person I loved on a journey from when we were with a loving Father in Heaven to when we can go home to him again. We would see the fall of Adam and Eve and feel its effects on us. We would go to Bethlehem and rejoice at the birth of the Son of God, and to the Garden and to Golgotha as our hearts break at the transcendent gift of the Atonement. And we would go to the open tomb, and to Galilee, and to this hemisphere to feel hope in keeping the commandments of a Risen Lord. Then we would go to a grove in New York to watch the boy Joseph Smith talk with God the Father and his resurrected Son, to begin the errand that restored the ordinances of the gospel, which can lead us home again.

President Clark understood that a person in whom faith is an ember won't receive even great teaching unless his heart is softened. And so he said that we must touch the person with the spirit of righteousness, with love, and with tenderness. Now, you and I might rightly feel that what he asks is nearly superhuman. In our efforts to invite others back, we may have felt rejection and even ridicule. We may feel fatigue, frustration, and sometimes guilt. How, then, can we keep reaching out in a spirit of righteousness, with love and tenderness?

The best answer I know comes from another wonderful father. His name was Mormon. He wrote a letter to his son Moroni in a time when they met not only rejection but unbridled hatred, and faced not only frustration but almost certain failure. Mormon wanted Moroni to meet even such a test with love and tenderness and the spirit of righteousness. He gave a formula, the same one given by true prophets in all ages. It has always worked. The promise is sure. Here it is, from Mormon's letter: "And the first fruits of repentance is baptism; and baptism cometh by faith unto the fulfilling the commandments; and the fulfilling the commandments bringeth remission of sins; and the remission of sins bringeth meekness, and lowliness of heart; and because of meekness and lowliness of heart cometh the visitation of the Holy Ghost, which Comforter filleth with hope and perfect love, which love endureth by diligence unto prayer, until the end shall come, when all the saints shall dwell with God." (Moroni 8:25–26.)

If you try to imagine the Savior restoring a lost sheep to the fold, won't you picture him cradling it in his arms? That tenderness and love, Mormon testifies to his son, is the natural result of the atonement of Jesus Christ operating in our lives. Our faith leads us to repentance, to the gifts of the Spirit, and from that to the perfect love which the Master Shepherd has, and knows we must have to serve Him.

The effects of the Atonement in our lives can also produce in us the example those we love will need. I learned again not long ago the example we need to be.

I was chatting with my wife at the end of a long day. Three of our children were in the room, listening. I turned and noticed that one of them was watching me—and watching my face intently. And then he asked me, softly,

"Why are you unhappy?" I tried to give a reason for my furrowed brow, but I realized later that he could well have been asking this deeper question: "Can I see in you the hope for peace in this life that Jesus promised?"

To turn my thoughts from what darkened my look to what would brighten it, I went to another letter from Mormon to his son. Both Mormon and Moroni were facing days of difficulty that make my challenges pale. Mormon knew his son might be overcome with gloom and foreboding, so he told him the perfect antidote. He told him that he could choose, by what he put in his mind, to become an example of hope. Here is what he wrote: "My son, be faithful in Christ; and may not the things which I have written grieve thee, to weigh thee down unto death; but may Christ lift thee up, and may his sufferings and death, and the showing his body unto our fathers, and his mercy and long-suffering, and the hope of his glory and of eternal life, rest in your mind forever." (Moroni 9:25.)

What we can do to help—teaching, and doing it with the spirit of righteousness, with love, with tenderness, with example—centers on the Savior and his atonement. That is what we would teach. The Atonement working in our lives will produce in us the love and tenderness we need. And by remembering him and his gift, which we promise to do as we take the sacrament each week, we can put a light of hope in our faces which those we love need so much to see.

President Clark reminded us, at the end of his suggestions, that there is, and always will be, agency. The spark won't glow brighter until the person tries living the gospel. That is why we hope so much that those we love will be called and will fulfill some assignment, however small. After their choice to serve others, to sacrifice, to try the commandments with promise, the spark of faith ignites.

Even after we have done all we can do, that choice—whether to act on what faith they have—must be theirs.

I bear my testimony that we have in this dispensation the power to offer again the full blessings of the gospel of Jesus Christ. And I pray that we may never cease to offer those blessings to those in whom the spark of faith may yet be fanned to flame.

HELPING A STUDENT IN A MOMENT OF DOUBT

If you are a teacher of youth in the Church, my heart goes out to you in gratitude and in admiration for your service. I share with you a love of teaching. In my travels across the Church, whenever someone is introduced to me as "our early-morning seminary teacher" or "our Mia Maid adviser" or "our teenager's Sunday School teacher," I hear a note of gratitude and admiration. I hope you can feel it also from the Saints whose lives you touch.

I suppose what keeps you going, even more than gratitude and admiration, is the glimpse you get of what a difference it can make when you teach well. You sometimes see it in the face of a former student reporting a successful mission or sitting in church with the person he or she married in the temple. It is then that you see what Mormon saw after he had recounted the journeying and the suffering of the people of Ammon: "And thus we see the great call of diligence of men to labor in the vineyards of the Lord; and

---

From an address to CES Religious Educators, 5 February 1993.

thus we see the great reason of sorrow, and also of rejoicing—sorrow because of death and destruction among men,
and joy because of the light of Christ unto life." (Alma
28:14.)

The fact that what you do matters both urges you on
and, at times, can be a discouragement. It can discourage
because, while you see the great consequences of the judgments and choices your students are making, sometimes
they do not see nearly as clearly. And that can tear at your
heart.

When I was serving as a bishop many years ago, a young
woman in my ward came for an interview. We somehow got
around to her telling me her feelings about her patriarchal
blessing. She said that it depressed her rather than helped
her. I must have looked surprised, because she explained her
feelings. She said that her blessing warned her about serious sin. And, at least by her report, it did little else. It
apparently warned her by describing a situation in which
she might find herself, and in which, if she yielded to temptation, she would come to great harm and sorrow. She said
that it hurt her in two ways: not only did it dwell on something depressing when she needed encouragement, but it
reminded her that her social life then was so barren that
such a situation could never arise. Our entire exchange
about the patriarchal blessing could not have lasted more
than a minute or two during our interview. But what struck
me was the tone in her voice. It was the sad sound of
doubt—not just doubt that her patriarch had been inspired,
but doubt that any ordinary human being, including me,
might actually speak words for God. I do not remember
what I said as I tried to help her that day. I remember the
feeling I had of wanting to do something.

I remember better the interview I had with her less than
a year later. She sobbed for a while, sitting in a chair on the

other side of my desk in the bishop's office. And then she blurted out her tragedy and how it had happened, exactly as the patriarch had described it years before. In her little season of doubt, that a patriarch could see with inspiration, she had made choices that led to years of sorrow.

The choices our students make, the ones that matter most, take faith. The right choice takes believing in things they cannot prove with logic or with evidence they can see with their natural eyes. It is not easy to believe that your neighbor, unschooled and imperfect, could really be a patriarch called of God—that he could really see future choices and future consequences for you, someone he hardly knows, who will live in future conditions foreign to the patriarch's experience.

Paul put the problem just right: "Now faith is the substance of things hoped for, the evidence of things not seen." (Hebrews 1:1.) And Moroni put it almost the same way: "Faith is things which are hoped for and not seen." (Ether 12:6.)

I would like to discuss how we can best help in those moments of quiet crisis in the lives of our students when they cannot see. The moment comes when they say to themselves, "Maybe what I thought was true, what I have depended upon, isn't so." And you may be the person they will turn to in such moments.

Picture yourself: You are sitting somewhere, a young person comes in with a sober look, the conversation begins, and then he or she says, "I just don't believe it anymore." For some reason, the picture that comes to my mind is of a nineteen-year-old boy sitting in a chair before me. He has on a short-sleeved sport shirt, because it is still fairly warm in California in November. He is a freshman, just months into a course called "Western Civilization." Before he even says a few words, I know what will come next. A professor, or maybe a graduate student leading his discussion section, has told him something about God, or about people who have claimed to be prophets or who have claimed revelation, or maybe it was about the Church or about Joseph Smith. But whatever, the result will be that he feels doubts—doubts about things he thought were true, doubts that seem now to have knocked out the props that had held up his world.

You may have a picture in your mind of someone who has come to you in such a crisis. Young people have these moments partly because they are growing up, trying to become independent, and sometimes choosing to question spiritual things as their way to break free. Whatever the reason for the moment of doubt, may I share with you what has seemed to me to help them most?

The key for me is to believe Paul and Moroni: faith is evidence of things not seen with natural eyes. And so doubt comes from a failure of spiritual sight. If you and I will be helpful to these young people, it will be to help them restore that sight. Just accepting such a simple picture will change the way I start the conversation; I will let them talk, not just about their doubts but also about their feelings. There are good reasons for that patient approach.

If you listen carefully to their feelings, you will find out something about the heart. Now, you might say, "But if the problem is sight, why do I want to know about the heart instead of testing their sight? If I want to help their spiritual sight, shouldn't I be trying to find out what they see and what they don't see?"

Well, no, because spiritual sight seems to depend on the heart. The Lord has taught us that many times. One of my favorite examples is the way he taught Joseph Smith to help Martin Harris. I suppose I love this story because I can feel the pain Martin must have felt when he struggled to rise to

138

the spiritual tasks the Lord was willing to let him undertake. He wanted to serve, but he faltered; he had doubts. This is how the Lord told Joseph to help him:

> And now, again, I speak unto you, my servant Joseph, concerning the man that desires the witness—behold, I say unto him, he exalts himself and does not humble himself sufficiently before me; but if he will bow down before me, and humble himself in mighty prayer and faith, in the sincerity of his heart, then will I grant unto him a view of the things which he desires to see. And then he shall say unto the people of this generation: Behold, I have seen the things which the Lord hath shown unto Joseph Smith, Jun., and I know of a surety that they are true, for I have seen them, for they have been shown unto me by the power of God and not of man. (D&C 5:23–25.)

"Faith, in the sincerity of his heart" was the requirement to view what God would show him by a power he could know was not of man. That is why I think you should listen to your doubting student first—and listen hard—to find out the state of the heart far more than the content of the mind. What seems to have hardened his or her heart? What softened it in the past? What might soften it now?

Once you have tried to answer those questions through listening, you are ready to set about trying to soften the heart. I have watched that done a variety of ways. In my observation, the least effective way is to go at it as if you could do the softening yourself. The better way is to ask yourself, "What has he said, or what have I felt, that gives me a clue as to what might make him decide that he wants to have a softened heart?" That must have been what Alma understood when he was preaching among the poor. You remember what he said: "Therefore, blessed are they who humble themselves without being compelled to be humble; or rather, in other words, blessed is he that believeth in the word of God, and is baptized without stubbornness of heart, yea, without being brought to know the word, or even compelled to know, before they will believe. Yea, there are many who do say: If thou wilt show unto us a sign from heaven, then we shall know of a surety; then we shall believe." (Alma 32:16–17.)

That last line may not be exactly what you will hear your students say as they describe their doubts, but all my experience says that it will be close. Since the young person before you has hit a moment when he doubts whether people can see things clearly with spiritual eyes, it is not surprising that what he thinks he needs is proof—either some visible evidence or some iron-clad logic. You will not often hear anything so blatant as what Korihor said, but you will feel the sense of what he said:

> And ye also say that Christ shall come. But behold, I say that ye do not know that there shall be a Christ. And ye say also that he shall be slain for the sins of the world—
>
> And thus ye lead away this people after the foolish traditions of your fathers, and according to your own desires; and ye keep them down, even as it were in bondage, that ye may glut yourselves with the labors of their hands, that they durst not look up with boldness, and that they durst not enjoy their rights and privileges.
>
> Yea, they durst not make use of that which is their own lest they should offend their priests, who do yoke them according to their desires, and have brought them to believe, by their traditions and their dreams and their whims and their visions and their pretended mysteries, that they should, if they did not do according to their words, offend some unknown being, who they say is God—a being who never has been seen or known, who never was nor ever will be. (Alma 30:26–28.)

You may not be attacked so directly and with that accusation of oppression. Your student may not say that there has been trickery to exert and exploit power. That generally comes after years of doubt, when the heart becomes hardened. But even in the very young, you will sense that their doubt is leading them that way. With or without the accusation of oppression, there will be a demand, or at least a plea, for evidence, for some proof. It may be words like this: "Please, give me some reason for the faith I once had."

In your love for your students, you may decide to try to give them what they ask. You may be tempted to go with them through their doubts, with the hope that you can find proof or reasoning to dispel their doubts. Persons with doubts often want to talk about what they think are the facts or the arguments that have caused their doubts, and about how much it hurts. They may well want to explore some scientific theory, some historical study, some political position, or some reported failures in the leaders of the Church or in its members, which they see as the source of their doubts.

Many good people have spent effort, and some have spent much of their lives, providing such exploration. Some have written scholarly books. Others have organized various meetings and other exchanges to allow those with questions and doubts to discuss them, with the hope that the doubts will be resolved. I admire their intent and their effort. But my observation is that the chance of success of such approaches, based on what scholars consider evidence and reason, is severely limited.

At the worst, exchanges between those who doubt will increase doubt. That will be true even if they are true seekers, simply because they will be introduced to new doubts. More than that, in any such group, if it is very large, there will be some impressive and sympathetic people who have made wrestling with doubts a major personal adventure. They will present it as sport, both exhilarating and noble.

Staying with such a bold band of inquirers, fearlessly confronting hard questions, can seem more attractive than moving back to the apparently less colorful company of quiet believers.

But even at its best, the resolution of doubts by reason and appeal to evidence cannot take us far. It is helpful to meet a brilliant mind who defends gospel truths with fact and logic. There is comfort in finding that such a person has confronted the same questions with which you struggle and has retained his faith. But there is a hazard. Even the most brilliant and faithful person may defend the truth with argument or fact that later proves false. The best scholarship has, at least, incompleteness in it. But even flawless argument has a weakness if you come to depend on it: What happens to the next doubt, or the next? What if no physical evidence or persuasive logic can be produced to dispel it? You will find then what I have found—that faithful scholar who reassured you with logic did not base his faith there. It was the other way around. His faith reassured him that someday, when God told him how it was all done, he would see all truth as perfectly logical, transparently reasonable. In the meantime he was enjoying discovering what he could with the logic he could muster.

My counsel to you is to look for a more powerful way to help your doubting students. I believe this sweet counsel from President Ezra Taft Benson:

> When a teacher feels he must blend worldly sophistication and erudition to the simple principles of the gospel or to our Church history so that his message will have more appeal and respectability to the academically learned, he has compromised his message. We seldom impress people by this means and almost never convert them to the gospel. This also applies to our students. We encourage you to get your higher degrees and to further your education; but let us not forget

that disaffection from the gospel and the Lord's church was brought about in the past by the attempts to reconcile the pure gospel with the secular philosophies of men. Nominal Christianity outside the restored church stands as an evidence that the blend between worldly philosophy and revealed truth leads to impotence. Likewise, you teachers will have no power if you attempt to do the same in your educational pursuits and classroom teaching. ("The Gospel Teacher and His Message," Address to Religious Educators, 17 September 1976, p. 8.)

You and I can do better if we do not stay long with what our students see as the source of their doubts. We must listen long enough to show that we care, that we understand, and that we are not troubled by what troubles them. But their problem does not lie in what they think they see; it lies in what they cannot yet see. Think about that a moment—*their problem does not lie in what they think they see; it lies in what they cannot yet see*. And so we do best if we turn the conversation soon to the things of the heart, those changes of the heart that open spiritual eyes.

As nearly as I can tell, you cannot help someone choose to have a softer heart unless he or she feels your love. That is hard, especially if you feel a knot of anger or fear inside you as you listen to the doubts spilled out, sometimes with tears, but more often with a touch of defiance.

The best help that ever came to me for that moment came on a night years ago when President Marion G. Romney spoke to a group of teachers in the Church Educational System. I was his host that night. He began his talk by saying: "Because this assignment to speak to you professional teachers about how to teach the gospel of Jesus Christ in these Church institutions requires an endowment which I do not possess, I shall say what I think should be said in the words President J. Reuben Clark, Jr., used in an address he gave forty-two years ago entitled 'The Charted Course of the Church in Education.'" ("The Charted Course Reaffirmed," Address to Religious Educators, 12 September 1980, p. 1.)

Then President Romney simply read President Clark's talk and added only one sentence of his own in closing. That was the end of his talk. I knew he had prepared a talk of his own, but he chose to read "The Charted Course of the Church in Education."

President Romney had no family member with him that night, so I volunteered to drive him to his house, about twenty minutes away. His talk, and the twenty minutes of private tutorial on the trip to his home, increased the confidence I feel when I reach out to help a student who feels doubt about gospel truths. Here is what happened in my tutorial: After we had driven along for a few minutes, I asked, "President Romney, don't you think young people and the world have changed almost completely since President Clark gave that talk in 1938?" And then I paraphrased what seemed, at least to me, a remarkable part of President Clark's talk:

> The youth of the Church are hungry for things of the Spirit; they are eager to learn the gospel, and they want it straight, undiluted. They want to know about the fundamentals I have just set out—about our beliefs; they want to gain testimonies of their truth. They are not now doubters but inquirers, seekers after truth. Doubt must not be planted in their hearts. Great is the burden and the condemnation of any teacher who sows doubt in a trusting soul.
>
> These students crave the faith their fathers and mothers have; they want it in its simplicity and purity. There are few indeed who have not seen the manifestations of its divine power. They wish to be not only the beneficiaries of this faith, but they want to be themselves able to call it forth to work.

("The Charted Course of the Church in Education," Address to Religious Educators, 8 August 1938, p. 3.)

I talked with President Romney, as we drove along, about all the changes in morals, in science, in education, in the sophistication of young people, and the changes in their families—and on and on. And that is when I repeated my question to him: "Do you think what President Clark taught still describes the way we should approach our students today?"

President Romney chuckled, sat silent for a moment, and then said, "Oh, I think President Clark could see our time—and beyond."

With that assurance, which the Spirit confirmed to me that night was true, it is easy to see the student sitting in front of you not as a doubter, but as a seeker after truth. You can ignore the attitude of challenge and see instead a person who craves faith, who has seen manifestations of divine power, even if he has not recognized them, and who wants not just to believe in those powers but to call them forth in his own life.

Now, President Clark did not say that you will never encounter someone who is hardened or even antagonistic. In fact, as a Relief Society president or a bishop, you may someday have to remove a diabolical doubter, just as Ammon had Korihor carried to the edge of town. Korihor could not be allowed to spread the cancer of his doubt, or the responsibility would have been Ammon's. But the rest of the story tells you what works and what does not work to help the doubter. Korihor got what he thought he needed, a physical sign—he was struck dumb. But you remember what Alma taught us and taught him: the terrible evidence of even that rebuke did not change Korihor's heart. Now, Korihor may have been past helping, but if we still have even a hope of helping an individual, it must be the hope that there is a glimmer of faith on which he may choose to act. That is the hope you feel in President Clark's optimistic counsel.

We can talk with our students as if they want to see the spiritual things by which they have been surrounded but which are now out of their view. We can treat them as seekers who would want a softened heart if it would allow them to see spiritual truth.

I can make a promise to you: if you treat them as seekers, they will feel that you love them, and that may awaken a hope in them that they could have a softer heart. It may not happen every time, and it may not last. But it will happen often, and sometimes it will last. And all of them will at least remember that you believed in the best in them— their inheritance as children of God.

President Clark's counsel gives you and me encouragement and direction in how to begin, how to shape those conversations with our students. Think of yourself sitting across from a student now. You have listened long and well enough that he knows you intend to treat him as an honest seeker. Now you will begin to talk quietly with him, acting as if he has the particle of faith described in this passage from Alma that you have read and taught so often: "Behold, if ye will awake and arouse your faculties, even to an experiment upon my words, and exercise a particle of faith, yea, even if ye can no more than desire to believe, let this desire work in you, even until ye believe in a manner that ye can give place for a portion of my words." (Alma 32:27.) You will treat him as if he has that desire to believe.

Now, what will you do to make it more likely that he will try an experiment that leads to greater faith? President Benson told us what to do: "Your purpose is to increase testimony and faith in your students. Should you wonder how this is done, carefully study the Book of Mormon to see how Mormon did it with his 'and thus we see' passages." ("The Gospel Teacher and His Message," p. 9.)

Most of us have pondered those "we see" passages, looking for patterns. But because of President Benson's suggestion, I went back through them again, and I saw something new.

I had always thought that phrases like that were put in to show when an argument had reached a conclusion. I suppose I have read too many books in mathematics in which the theorem or a proof goes along for lines, or sometimes pages, proving this thing and then proving that thing, and then there is a line that begins with "thus we see" or sometimes "it is obvious," which generally means that what comes next has to be true if you accept what has already been proved up to that point.

What Mormon, Nephi, and Moroni were doing is like that, but different in a very important way. I must not pretend that I know all that they meant or what they did not mean. But for me there is this meaning, repeated time after time: The writer will have recounted an event or described some fact. It will not have been an argument; it will have been a description. And then we find the words "and thus we see" or "we see," followed by a statement of some spiritual truth, something about the way God deals with his children or what our life is like as God sees it.

What went before does not prove the conclusion in the way the world looks for evidence or logic. What went before is what someone with spiritual sight will observe and then say, "Oh, yes, now I see that." And then follows, after the "thus we see," what that someone would see. When I understood that, I realized how gracious the word *we* is in that phrase "and thus we see." The writer was saying, "I include you with me among those who see." Ever since then, each time I've read the words "we see" in the Book of Mormon, I have felt a warm burning for two reasons: first, I have felt included as a seeker and a believer by the writer, just as President Clark urged us to approach those we try to help; and second, I have felt the burning that tells me that the thing the writer could see was true.

You can best understand how the "thus we see" passages work by looking at an example in which one person could see and one could not. You remember the time: Captain Moroni had an army cornered. He could have slaughtered them, but instead he offered them freedom and their lives if they would surrender their arms and take an oath of peace. Here is what he said:

> Now ye see that this is the true faith of God; yea, ye see that God will support, and keep, and preserve us, so long as we are faithful unto him, and unto our faith, and our religion; and never will the Lord suffer that we shall be destroyed except we should fall into transgression and deny our faith.
>
> And now, Zerahemnah, I command you, in the name of that all-powerful God, who has strengthened our arms that we have gained power over you, by our faith, by our religion, and by our rites of worship, and by our church, and by the sacred support which we owe to our wives and our children, by that liberty which binds us to our lands and our country; yea, and also by the maintenance of the sacred word of God, to which we owe all our happiness; and by all that is most dear unto us—
>
> Yea, and this is not all; I command you by all the desires which ye have for life, that ye deliver up your weapons of war unto us, and we will seek not your blood, but we will spare your lives, if ye will go your way and come not again to war against us. (Alma 44:4–6.)

Now, Zerahemnah had solid evidence for the proposition that something beyond human power had him where he faced annihilation. But did he see what Moroni saw, looking at the same set of facts? You remember his response: "We are not of your faith; we do not believe that it is God that has delivered us into your hands; but we believe that it is your cunning that has preserved you from our swords. Behold, it is your breastplates and your shields that have preserved you." (Alma 44:9.)

He could not see the true connection, because his heart was not soft enough, not changed enough, that the Holy Ghost could show it to him. And neither will your student until he or she chooses to do those things that bring that capacity to see.

The only sure way I know to soften a heart enough for that is to get the effects of the atonement of Jesus Christ into a person's life. So early in your interview you will find a way to bear testimony of the Savior; of the Fall, which demanded a Savior in order for us to go home to our Heavenly Father; of the Savior's mission; of his atonement; of his resurrection; and of his restoration of the Church through the Prophet Joseph.

We find the way it is done in a place where Alma was quoted by Mormon in another "and thus we see" passage. Alma was in an interview with a doubter, his son Corianton. As you read the early parts of the interview, you become sure that he had listened carefully to his son. Alma saw that Corianton had a question. Corianton doubted the justice of God; it seemed too severe because of his own sins. To those with unrepented sins, the truth always seems hard, so doubt is a natural defense. You will seldom know if sin is a major source of the doubt in the person before you, but whether it is or not, you will be wise to bear testimony not only of the justice of God but also of his mercy. You remember that Alma did it for his son this way: "And thus we see that all mankind were fallen, and they were in the grasp of justice; yea, the justice of God, which consigned them forever to be cut off from his presence. And now, the plan of mercy could not be brought about except an atonement should be made; therefore God himself atoneth for the sins of the world, to bring about the plan of mercy, to appease the demands of justice, that God might be a perfect, just God, and a merciful God also." (Alma 42:14–15.)

Alma was not offering proof. He was offering testimony of the kindness and mercy of the Savior toward his errant, troubled son. He knew that his testimony, should it touch his son, might lead him to try the experiment to gain the faith and thus the forgiveness and the softening he would need to return to his labors.

We may be tempted to be too indirect in our bearing of testimony. You do not have to speak loudly or long. But you must be clear. President Gordon B. Hinckley put that as plainly as it can be put. He said:

> Teach faith in Jesus Christ, the Son of God, the Word that was made flesh and dwelt among us, the only perfect life that was ever lived, the exemplar for all men, the Lamb who was sacrificed for the sins of the world, our Redeemer and our Savior.
>
> There is no need to try to justify, to equivocate, to rationalize, to enlarge, to explain. Why should we equivocate? Why should we rationalize? I give you these great words of Paul to Timothy: "For God hath not given us the spirit of fear; but of power, and of love, and of a sound mind. Be not thou therefore ashamed of the testimony of our Lord." (II Timothy 1:7–8.)
>
> I wish every member of this institution would print that and put it on his mirror where he would see it every morning as he begins his day. "Be not thou therefore ashamed of the testimony of our Lord."
>
> Teach the simple, straightforward truth that came out of the vision of the boy Joseph Smith. Teach the reality of that vision and the manifestations that followed, that brought into being the restored Church of Jesus Christ—the Church

of Jesus Christ of Latter-day Saints. ("What Shall You Teach?" Address to Brigham Young University Faculty and Staff, 17 September 1963, p. 5.)

When you see a spark, a response to your testimony, you will urge your students to try the experiment of doing something through which they can taste the fruit for themselves. That is the evidence they need.

I, at least, would begin urging fervent prayer and searching of the scriptures. Most of the young people you talk with about their doubts will say they are praying and studying. They may be praying, and they may be reading scriptures. But if you can learn more of what they are doing, you will often find that they are not doing it the way that works. You may have to find a moment that fits the person and his mood, but you can help him learn how to obtain the sure result which the Lord promises if we approach him in the right way: "Thus we may see that the Lord is merciful unto all who will, in the sincerity of their hearts, call upon his holy name. Yea, thus we see that the gate of heaven is open unto all, even to those who will believe on the name of Jesus Christ, who is the Son of God. Yea, we see that whosoever will may lay hold upon the word of God, which is quick and powerful, which shall divide asunder all the cunning and the snares and the wiles of the devil, and lead the man of Christ in a strait and narrow course across that everlasting gulf of misery which is prepared to engulf the wicked." (Helaman 3:27–29.)

Perhaps not in the first interview, but soon, you will urge your students to go beyond prayer and scripture study. You will testify to them, as I now testify to you, that the effect of sincere prayer and of careful scripture study is to *always* feel an urging to *do* things. You must tell them, bearing testimony from your own experience, that they need to make a choice simply to be obedient. Real spiritual sight comes to the heart softened by obedience. It takes time, but it is the sure way to see. The Lord made that clear, at least to you and to me, when he said: "My doctrine is not mine, but his that sent me. If any man will do his will, he shall know of the doctrine, whether it be of God, or whether I speak of myself." (John 7:16–17.)

Perhaps the largest set of "and thus we see" passages teaches and encourages the simple keeping of the commandments. Let us start with a passage so familiar it is almost a signature for Mormon's teaching found in Alma: "And thus we see how merciful and just are all the dealings of the Lord, to the fulfilling of all his words unto the children of men; yea, we can behold that his words are verified, even at this time, which he spake unto Lehi, saying: Blessed art thou and thy children; and they shall be blessed, inasmuch as they shall keep my commandments they shall prosper in the land. But remember, inasmuch as they will not keep my commandments they shall be cut off from the presence of the Lord." (Alma 50:19–20.)

Nephi gave us similar encouragement. He said that if you just start, however hard the commandment seems to be, God will strengthen you: "And thus we see that the commandments of God must be fulfilled. And if it so be that the children of men keep the commandments of God he doth nourish them, and strengthen them, and provide means whereby they can accomplish the thing which he has commanded them; wherefore, he did provide means for us while we did sojourn in the wilderness." (1 Nephi 17:3.)

Along with the encouragement there is a warning. You owe giving it to your student when he or she is ready. Mormon pointed out that the promise works in both directions. And our students will need that to understand not only what they must do to gain faith, but why doubt is a natural consequence of choices, just as faith is:

> And they did grow in their iniquities in the sixty and eighth year also, to the great sorrow and lamentation of the righteous.
>
> And thus we see that the Nephites did begin to dwindle in unbelief, and grow in wickedness and abominations, while the Lamanites began to grow exceedingly in the knowledge of their God; yea, they did begin to keep his statutes and commandments, and to walk in truth and uprightness before him.
>
> And thus we see that the Spirit of the Lord began to withdraw from the Nephites, because of the wickedness and the hardness of their hearts.
>
> And thus we see that the Lord began to pour out his Spirit upon the Lamanites, because of their easiness and willingness to believe in his words.
>
> And it came to pass that the Lamanites did hunt the band of robbers of Gadianton; and they did preach the word of God among the more wicked part of them, insomuch that this band of robbers was utterly destroyed from among the Lamanites.
>
> And it came to pass on the other hand, that the Nephites did build them up and support them, beginning at the more wicked part of them, until they had overspread all the land of the Nephites, and had seduced the more part of the righteous until they had come down to believe in their works and partake of their spoils, and to join with them in their secret murders and combinations.
>
> And thus they did obtain the sole management of the government, insomuch that they did trample under their feet and smite and rend and turn their backs upon the poor and the meek, and the humble followers of God.
>
> And thus we see that they were in an awful state, and ripening for an everlasting destruction. (Helaman 6:33–40.)

Somewhere in the conversations you will have with doubting students, you need to let them know at least one more thing. You have already let them sense that you deal with them as honest seekers. You need to let them know something else that will help. You ought to let them know that the spiritual experiences they need do not come from a God who is distant. When anyone doubts, the feeling is of being alone. So it is easy for Satan to whisper that God is hard to reach. But you must teach your students that that is not true. You can tell them the Lord's own words: "Behold, I stand at the door, and knock: if any man hear my voice, and open the door, I will come in to him, and will sup with him, and he with me." (Revelation 3:20.)

I testify to you that that is true. He is not hard to reach. He reaches out. He invites us. He is patient. And he knows us personally.

You need to exemplify optimism. Not only can you treat every student as a seeker who hopes for a testimony of the truth, and one who has had spiritual experience, but you can be confident that the Savior is reaching out, eager to respond when that student seeks him. Your students will then feel your faith, and that will bolster theirs.

What we have talked about is simple, but it is not easy. The Lord knew that when he invited you to this labor. That is why he called for diligence and told you how much it matters: "And thus we see how great the inequality of man is because of sin and transgression, and the power of the devil, which comes by the cunning plans which he hath devised to ensnare the hearts of men. And thus we see the great call of diligence of men to labor in the vineyards of the Lord; and thus we see the great reason of sorrow, and also of rejoicing—sorrow because of death and destruction among men, and joy because of the light of Christ unto life." (Alma 28:13–14.)

I can promise you some things. First, about the Savior: He is reaching out. He will reach out to you, and he will reach out to your students as you try to help them. And second, about your students: They will respond when you treat them as honest seekers who want to believe. At least they will feel that you love them. And more than that, many of them will find their desire to believe increased. I can promise you that by hearing your testimony and the testimonies of those believers who wrote the scriptures, and from fervent prayer, they will feel a stirring in their hearts to believe in the Lord Jesus Christ. When they sincerely try to keep his commandments, when they conform to the ordinances, they will have the Atonement work in their lives. That will soften their hearts.

I testify to you that the sure effect of the Atonement is meekness and lowliness of heart, and from that comes the visitation of the Holy Ghost. And thus they will see. Then those students you love so much will, even in the hardest of times, be able to do what the Savior promised they could do: "Look unto me in every thought; doubt not, fear not." (D&C 6:36.)

I pray that you may be blessed to help your students, who want so much to see the things that give you peace and give you hope. I pray that you will act wisely and well. I pray that you will feel God's approval. He loves you. He appreciates what you do for his children, and he will bless you in this great service.

CHAPTER 13

THE FAMILY

Since the restoration of the gospel of Jesus Christ through the Prophet Joseph Smith until 23 September 1995, The Church of Jesus Christ of Latter-day Saints has issued a proclamation only four times. It has been more than fifteen years since the last one, which described the progress the Church had made in 150 years of its history. Thus, you can imagine the importance our Heavenly Father places upon the subject of this most recent proclamation.

Because our Father loves his children, he will not leave us to guess about what matters most in this life concerning where our attention could bring happiness or our indifference bring sadness. Sometimes he will tell a person directly, by inspiration. But he will, in addition, tell us through his servants. In the words of the prophet Amos, recorded long ago, "Surely the Lord God will do nothing, but he revealeth his secret unto his servants the prophets." (Amos 3:7.) He does that so that even those who cannot feel inspiration

From a talk given at a CES Fireside for College-Age Young Adults; Satellite Broadcast 5 November 1995, Brigham Young University.

can know, if they will only listen, that they have been told the truth and been warned.

The title of the proclamation reads: "The Family: A Proclamation to the World—The First Presidency and Council of the Twelve Apostles of The Church of Jesus Christ of Latter-day Saints." (See *Ensign*, Nov. 1995, p. 102.)

Three things about the title are worth our careful reflection. First, the subject: the family. Second, the audience, which is the whole world. And third, those who proclaimed are those we sustain as prophets, seers, and revelators. That means that the family must be as important to us as anything we can consider, that what the proclamation says could help anyone in the world, and that the proclamation fits the Lord's promise when he said, "Whether by mine own voice or by the voice of my servants, it is the same." (D&C 1:38.)

Before we start to listen to the words of the proclamation together, the title tells us something about how to prepare. We can expect that God won't just tell us a few interesting things about the family; he will tell us what a family ought to be and why. And we know at the outset that we could be easily overwhelmed with such thoughts as: "This is so high a standard and I am so weak that I can never hope for such a family." That feeling can come because what our Heavenly Father and his son Jesus Christ want for us is to become like them so that we can dwell with them forever, in families. We know that from this simple statement of their intent:

"This is my work and my glory—to bring to pass the immortality and eternal life of man." (Moses 1:39.)

Eternal life means to become like the Father and to live in families in happiness and joy forever, so of course what he wants for us will require help beyond our powers. That feeling of our inadequacy can make it easier to repent and to be ready to rely on the Lord's help.

The fact that the proclamation goes to all the world—to every person and government in it—gives us assurance that we need not be overwhelmed. Whoever we are, however difficult our circumstances, we can know that what our Father commands we do to qualify for the blessings of eternal life will not be beyond us. What a young boy said long ago when he faced a seemingly impossible assignment is true:

"I know that the Lord giveth no commandments unto the children of men, save he shall prepare a way for them that they may accomplish the thing which he commandeth them." (1 Nephi 3:7.)

We may have to pray with faith to know what we are to do and we must pray with a determination to obey, but we can know what to do and be sure that the way has been prepared for us by the Lord. As we read of what the proclamation tells us about the family, we can expect, in fact we must expect, impressions to come to our minds as to what we are to do, and we can be confident it is possible.

The proclamation begins this way:

"We, the First Presidency and the Council of the Twelve Apostles of The Church of Jesus Christ of Latter-day Saints, solemnly proclaim that marriage between a man and a woman is ordained of God and that the family is central to the Creator's plan for the eternal destiny of His children."

Try to imagine yourself as a little child, hearing those words for the first time, and believing that they are true. This can be a useful attitude whenever we read or hear the word of God because he has told us, "Verily I say unto you, Whosoever shall not receive the kingdom of God as a little child shall in no wise enter therein." (Luke 18:17.)

A little child would feel safe hearing the words that marriage between a man and woman is ordained of God. The child would know that the longing to have the love of both a father and a mother, distinct but somehow perfectly complementary, exists because that is the eternal pattern, the pattern of happiness. The child would also feel safer knowing that God would help mother and father resolve differences and love each other, if only they will ask for his help and try. Prayers of children across the earth would go up to God, pleading for his help for parents and for families.

Read in that same way, as if you were a little child, the next words of the proclamation:

"All human beings—male and female—are created in the image of God. Each is a beloved spirit son or daughter of heavenly parents, and, as such, each has a divine nature and destiny. Gender is an essential characteristic of individual premortal, mortal, and eternal identity and purpose.

"In the premortal realm, spirit sons and daughters knew and worshiped God as their Eternal Father and accepted His plan by which His children could obtain a physical body and gain earthly experience to progress toward perfection and ultimately realize his or her divine destiny as an heir of eternal life. The divine plan of happiness enables family relationships to be perpetuated beyond the grave. Sacred ordinances and covenants available in holy temples make it possible for individuals to return to the presence of God and for families to be united eternally."

Understanding these truths ought to make it easier for us to feel like a little child, not just as we read the proclamation, but throughout our lives, because we are children—but in what a family and of what parents! We can picture ourselves as we were, for longer than we can imagine, sons and daughters associating in our heavenly home

160

with parents who knew and loved us. But now we can see ourselves home again with our heavenly parents, in that wonderful place, not only as sons and daughters but husbands and wives, fathers and mothers, grandfathers and grandmothers, grandsons and granddaughters, bound together forever in loving families. And we know that in the premortal world we were men or women, with unique gifts because of our gender, and that the opportunity to be married and to become one was necessary for us to have eternal happiness.

With that picture before us we can never be tempted even to think, "Maybe I wouldn't like eternal life. Maybe I would be just as happy in some other place in the life after death. I've heard that even the lowest kingdoms are more beautiful than anything we have ever seen."

We must have the goal not just in our minds but in our hearts. What we want is eternal life in families. We don't just want it if that is what works out, nor do we want something approaching eternal life. We want eternal life, whatever its cost in effort, pain, and sacrifice. Whenever we are tempted to make eternal life our hope instead of our determination, we might think of a building I took a look at a few weeks ago.

I was in Boston. For a little nostalgia, I walked up to the front of the boarding house I was living in when I met Kathleen, who is now my wife. That was a long time ago, so I expected to find the house a little more dilapidated than it was, since I seem to be a little more dilapidated. But to our surprise, it was freshly painted and much renovated. A university has purchased it from the Sopers, the people who owned it and ran it as a boarding house.

The building was locked, so we couldn't get in to see the back room on the top floor, which once was mine. Costs have changed, so this will be hard for you to believe, but this was the deal the Sopers gave me: My own large room and bath, furniture and sheets provided, maid service, six big breakfasts and five wonderful dinners a week, at the price of $21 a week. More than that, the meals were ample and prepared with such skill that we called our landlady with some affection, "Ma Soper." Just talking about it with you makes me realize that I didn't thank Mrs. Soper often enough, nor Mr. Soper and their daughter, since it must have been some burden to have twelve single men to dinner every week night.

Now, you aren't tempted by that description of a boarding house, and neither am I. It could have the most spacious rooms, the best service, and the finest eleven men you could ever know as fellow boarders and we wouldn't want to live there for more than a short while. If it were beautiful beyond our power to imagine, we wouldn't want to live there forever, single, if we have even the dimmest memory or the faintest vision of a family with beloved parents and children, like the one from which we came to this earth and the one which is our destiny to form and to live in forever. There is only one place where there will be families— the highest degree of the celestial kingdom. That is where we will want to be.

A child hearing and believing those words would begin a lifetime of looking for a holy temple where ordinances and covenants perpetuate family relationships beyond the grave and would begin a striving to become worthy, and to find a potential mate who has become worthy, of such ordinances. The words of the proclamation make it clear that to receive those blessings requires some sort of perfecting experiences. A child might not sense at first, but soon would learn, that all the making of resolutions and trying harder can produce only faltering progress toward perfection. With age will come temptations to acts that create

162

feelings of guilt. Every child will someday feel those pangs of conscience, as we all have. And those who feel that priceless sense of guilt and cannot shake it may despair, sensing that eternal life requires a progress toward perfection that seems increasingly to be beyond them. So you and I will resolve to speak to someone who doesn't yet know what we know about how that perfection is produced. We will do that because we know that someday they will want what we want, and will then realize that we were their brother or sister, and that we knew the way to eternal life. Tonight and tomorrow it won't be hard to be a member missionary if you think of that future moment when they and we will see things as they really are.

Some other words in the proclamation will have special meaning for us, knowing what we know about eternal life. They are in the next two paragraphs:

"The first commandment that God gave to Adam and Eve pertained to their potential for parenthood as husband and wife. We declare that God's commandment for His children to multiply and replenish the earth remains in force. We further declare that God has commanded that the sacred powers of procreation are to be employed only between man and woman, lawfully wedded as husband and wife.

"We declare the means by which mortal life is created to be divinely appointed. We affirm the sanctity of life and of its importance to God's eternal plan."

Believing those words, a child could spot easily the mistakes in reasoning made by adults. For instance, apparently wise and powerful people blame poverty and famine on there being too many people in some parts of the earth or in all the earth. With great passion they argue for limiting births, as if that will produce human happiness. A child believing the proclamation will know that cannot be so,

163

even before hearing these words from the Lord through his prophet, Joseph Smith:

"For the earth is full, and there is enough and to spare; yea, I prepared all things, and have given unto the children of men to be agents unto themselves." (D&C 104:17.)

A child could see that Heavenly Father would not command men and women to marry and to multiply and replenish the earth if the children they invited into mortality would deplete the earth. Since there is enough and to spare, the enemy of human happiness as well as the cause of poverty and starvation is not the birth of children. It is the failure of people to do with the earth what God could teach them to do, if only they would ask and then obey, for they are agents unto themselves.

We would also see that the commandment to be chaste, to employ the powers of procreation only as husband and wife, is not limiting but rather expanding and exalting. Children are the inheritance of the Lord to us in this life, but also in eternity. Eternal life is not only to have forever our descendants from this life. It is also to have eternal increase. This is the description of what awaits those of us married as husband and wife by a servant of God with authority to offer us the sacred sealing ordinances. Here are the words of the Lord:

"It shall be done unto them in all things whatsoever my servant hath put upon them, in time, and through all eternity; and shall be of full force when they are out of the world; and they shall pass by the angels, and the gods, which are set there, to their exaltation and glory in all things, as hath been sealed upon their heads, which glory shall be a fulness and a continuation of the seeds forever and ever.

"Then shall they be gods, because they have no end;

therefore shall they be from everlasting to everlasting."
(D&C 132:19–20.)

Now you can see why our Father in Heaven puts such a
high standard before us in using procreative powers whose
continuation is at the heart of eternal life. He told us what
that was worth this way:

"And, if you keep my commandments and endure to
the end you shall have eternal life, which gift is the greatest
of all the gifts of God." (D&C 14:7.)

We can understand why our Heavenly Father commands us to reverence life and to cherish the powers that
produce it as sacred. If we do not have those feelings in this
life, how could our Father give them to us in the eternities?
Family life here is the schoolroom in which we prepare for
family life there. And to give us the opportunity for family
life there was and is the purpose of creation. That is why
the coming of Elijah was described this way:

"And he shall plant in the hearts of the children the
promises made to the fathers, and the hearts of the children
shall turn to their fathers. If it were not so, the whole earth
would be utterly wasted at his coming." (Joseph Smith—
History 1:39.)

For some of us, the test in that schoolroom of mortality
will be to want marriage and children in this life, with all
our hearts, but to have it delayed or denied. Even such a
sorrow can be turned to blessing by a just and loving Father
and his Son, Jesus Christ. No one who strives with full faith
and heart for the blessings of eternal life will be denied.
And how great will be the joy and how much deeper the
appreciation then after enduring in patience and faith now.

The proclamation describes our schooling here for family life in the presence of our Eternal Father:

"Husband and wife have a solemn responsibility to love
and care for each other and for their children. 'Children are

an heritage of the Lord' (Psalms 127:3). Parents have a sacred duty to rear their children in love and righteousness, to provide for their physical and spiritual needs, to teach them to love and serve one another, to observe the commandments of God and to be law-abiding citizens wherever they live. Husbands and wives—mothers and fathers—will be held accountable before God for the discharge of these obligations.

"The family is ordained of God. Marriage between man and woman is essential to His eternal plan. Children are entitled to birth within the bonds of matrimony, and to be reared by a father and a mother who honor marital vows with complete fidelity. Happiness in family life is most likely to be achieved when founded upon the teachings of the Lord Jesus Christ. Successful marriages and families are established and maintained on principles of faith, prayer, repentance, forgiveness, respect, love, compassion, work, and wholesome recreational activities. By divine design, fathers are to preside over their families in love and righteousness and are responsible to provide the necessities of life and protection for their families. Mothers are primarily responsible for the nurture of their children. In these sacred responsibilities, fathers and mothers are obligated to help one another as equal partners. Disability, death, or other circumstances may necessitate individual adaptation. Extended families should lend support when needed."

Those two paragraphs are filled with practical implications. There are things we can start to do now. They have to do with providing for the spiritual and the physical needs of a family. There are things we can do now to prepare, long before the need, so that we can be at peace knowing we have done all we can.

To begin with, we can decide to plan for success, not failure. Statistics are thrown at us every day to persuade us that a family composed of a loving father and mother with children loved, taught, and cared for in the way the proclamation enjoins is going the way of the dinosaurs, toward extinction. You have enough evidence in your own families that righteous people sometimes have their families ripped apart by circumstances beyond their control. It takes courage and faith to plan for what God holds before you as the ideal rather than what might be forced upon you by circumstances.

There are important ways in which planning for failure can make failure more likely and the ideal less so. Consider these twin commandments as an example: "Fathers are to . . . provide the necessities of life . . . for their families" and "mothers are primarily responsible for the nurture of their children." Knowing how hard that might be, a young man might choose a career on the basis of how much money he could make, even if it meant he couldn't be home enough to be an equal partner. By doing that, he has already decided he cannot hope to do what would be best. A young woman might prepare for a career incompatible with being primarily responsible for the nurture of her children because of the possibilities of not marrying, of not having children, or of being left alone to provide for them herself. Or, she might fail to focus her education on the gospel and the knowledge of the world that nurturing a family would require, not realizing that the highest and best use she could make of her talents and her education would be in her home. Because a young man and woman had planned to take care of the worst, they might make the best less likely.

They are both wise to worry about the physical needs of that future family. The costs of buying a home, compared to average salaries, seem to be rising and jobs harder to hold. But there are other ways the young man and the young woman could think tonight about preparing to

167

provide for that future family. Income is only part of it. Have you noticed husbands and wives who feel pinched for lack of money, then choose ways to make their family income keep rising, and then find that the pinch is there whatever the income? There is an old formula you've heard, which goes something like this: Income five dollars and expenses six dollars: misery. Income four dollars and expenses three dollars: happiness.

Whether the young man can provide and still be in the home and whether the young woman can be there to nurture children can depend as much on how they learn to spend as how they learn to earn. Brigham Young said it this way, speaking to us as much as he did to the people in his day:

"If you wish to get rich, save what you get. A fool can earn money; but it takes a wise man to save and dispose of it to his own advantage. Then go to work, and save everything, and make your own bonnets and clothing." (*Journal of Discourses*, 11:201.)

In today's world, instead of telling you to make bonnets, he might suggest you think carefully about what you really need in cars, and clothes, and recreation, and houses, and vacations, and whatever else you will someday try to provide for your children. And he might point out that the difference in cost between what the world tells you is necessary and what your children really need could allow you the margin in time that a father and a mother might need with their children to bring them home to their Heavenly Father.

Even the most frugal spending habits and the most careful planning for employment may not be enough to ensure success, but it could be enough to allow you the peace that comes from knowing you did the best you could to provide and to nurture.

There is another way we could plan to succeed tonight, despite the difficulties that might lie before us. The proclamation sets a high hurdle for us to clear when it describes our obligation to teach our children. We are somehow to teach them so that they love one another and serve one another and keep the commandments and are law-abiding citizens. If we think of good families who have not met that test, and few meet it without some degree of failure over a generation or two, we could lose heart.

We cannot control what others choose to do, and so we cannot force our children to heaven, but we can determine what we will do. And we can decide tonight that we will do all we can to bring down the powers of heaven into that family we want so much to have forever.

A key for us is in the proclamation in this sentence: "Happiness in family life is most likely to be achieved when founded upon the teachings of the Lord Jesus Christ."

What could make it more likely that people in a family would love and serve one another, observe the commandments of God, and obey the law? It is not simply teaching them the gospel. It is in their hearing the word of God and then trying it in faith. If they do, their natures will be changed in a way that produces the happiness we seek. From Moroni these words describe exactly how that change is the natural fruit of living the gospel of Jesus Christ:

"And the first fruits of repentance is baptism; and baptism cometh by faith unto the fulfilling the commandments; and the fulfilling the commandments bringeth remission of sins;

"And the remission of sins bringeth meekness, and lowliness of heart; and because of meekness and lowliness of heart cometh the visitation of the Holy Ghost, which Comforter filleth with hope and perfect love, which love endureth by diligence unto prayer, until the end shall come,

169

when all the saints shall dwell with God" (Moroni 8:25–26).

When we prepare children for baptism, if we do it well, we prepare them for the process that will bring the effects of the Atonement into their lives and the powers of heaven into our home. Think of the change we need. We need the Holy Ghost to fill us with hope and perfect love, so that we can endure by diligence unto prayer. And then we can dwell forever with God in families. How can it come? By the simple promise Mormon described to his son Moroni. Faith in Jesus Christ unto repentance and then baptism by those with authority leads to remission of sins. And that produces meekness and lowliness of heart. And that in turn allows us to have the companionship of the Holy Ghost, which fills us with hope and perfect love.

You know that is true; I know that is true from our own experience and from the experience of those in our families. We know that someday we could find on our bedspread, after a twenty-hour flight across the world, a sign written in colors in a childish hand: "You must be so tired! Lie down and relax! You're back home where we'll take care of everything!" And you could know that is more than talk if her older sister had said in a phone call made at a stopping place on that flight home, "Oh, I'm just vacuuming the house."

How does an eleven-year-old who has never flown across the sea know the effects of jet lag on her mother and father? How does a fifteen-year-old decide to run a vacuum without being asked? Or how does a husband know the feelings of his wife, or a wife the feelings of her husband, and so understand without being told, and then help without being asked? Why does a niece give up her bed to an aunt and a nephew share his house and dinner table? How does a son and a daughter-in-law find it possible to take children into their already busy home and act as if it were a blessing? It takes the powers of heaven brought down by believing these words, and acting upon them:

"And the remission of sins bringeth meekness, and lowliness of heart; and because of meekness and lowliness of heart cometh the visitation of the Holy Ghost, which Comforter filleth with hope and perfect love, which love endureth by diligence unto prayer, until the end shall come, when all the saints shall dwell with God." (Moroni 8:26.) And may I add the words "in families."

The proclamation is careful in what it promises: "happiness in family life is most likely to be achieved when founded upon the teachings of the Lord Jesus Christ." My heart aches a little to know that many who read those words will be surrounded by those who do not know or who deny the teachings of Jesus Christ. They can only do their best. But, they can know this: their placement in a family, however challenging, is known by a loving Heavenly Father. They can know that a way is prepared for them to do all that will be required for them to qualify for eternal life. They may not see how God could give them that gift, nor with whom they will share it. Yet the promise of the gospel of Jesus Christ is sure:

"But learn that he who doeth the works of righteousness shall receive his reward, even peace in this world, and eternal life in the world to come.

"I, the Lord, have spoken it, and the Spirit beareth record. Amen." (D&C 59:23–24.)

That peace will come from the assurance that the Atonement has worked in our lives and the hope of eternal life that springs from it.

The proclamation warns that for those who fail to respond the result will be more disastrous than simply lack of peace in this life or absence of happiness. Here is the prophetic warning and the call to action, with which the proclamation ends:

"We warn that individuals who violate covenants of chastity, who abuse spouse or offspring, or who fail to fulfill family responsibilities will one day stand accountable before God. Further, we warn that the disintegration of the family will bring upon individuals, communities, and nations the calamities foretold by ancient and modern prophets.

"We call upon responsible citizens and officers of government everywhere to promote those measures designed to maintain and strengthen the family as the fundamental unit of society."

The family unit is not only fundamental to society and to the Church but to our hope for eternal life. We begin to practice in the family, the smaller unit, what will spread to the Church and to the society in which we live in this world, and then will be what we practice in families bound together forever by covenants and by faithfulness. We can start now to "promote those measures designed to maintain and strengthen the family." I pray that we will. I pray that you will ask, "Father, how can I prepare?" Tell him how much you want what it is that he wants so much to give you. You will receive impressions, and if you act on them, I promise you the help of the powers of heaven.

I testify that our Heavenly Father lives, that we lived with him as spirits, and that we would be lonely living anywhere but with him in the world to come.

I testify that Jesus Christ is our Savior, that he made possible the changes in you and me that can give us eternal life by suffering for the sins of all of us, his spirit brothers and sisters, the children of his Heavenly Father and our Heavenly Father.

I testify that the Holy Ghost can fill us with hope and with perfect love.

And I testify that the sealing power restored to Joseph Smith and now held by President Gordon B. Hinckley can bind us in families and give us eternal life, if we do all that we can do in faith.

CHAPTER 14

A LEGACY OF
TESTIMONY

We want for our families what God wants for them: that they will live in love and righteousness. But in our thoughtful moments we know that we will need help. We will need to invite the powers of heaven to guide our families in days when we are not there and to face spiritual dangers we may not foresee.

Our families can be given a gift to know what God would have them do and to learn it in a way that will encourage them to do it. God has provided such a guide. It is the Holy Ghost. We cannot give that to our family members as a companion, but they can earn it. The Holy Ghost can be their constant companion only after they have been faithful and after they have received the ordinances of baptism and the laying on of hands by those with proper authority. But even before baptism, children or adults can have the Holy Ghost testify to their hearts of sacred truth. They must act on that testimony to retain it, but it will guide them toward goodness, and it can lead them to accept

From a talk given at General Conference, 7 April 1996.

and keep the covenants which will in time bring them the companionship of the Holy Ghost.

We would, if we could, leave our families a legacy of testimony that it might reach through the generations. What we can do to create and transmit that legacy comes from an understanding of how testimony is instilled in our hearts. Since it is the Holy Ghost who testifies of sacred truth, we can do at least three things to make that experience more likely for our families. First, we can teach some sacred truth. Then we can testify that we know what we have taught is true. And finally we must act so that those who hear our testimony see that our actions conform with what we said was true. The Holy Ghost will then confirm to them the truth of what we said and that we knew it to be true.

That is how a legacy of testimony is created, preserved, and transmitted in a family. It isn't easy, but ordinary people have done it. Like many of you, I had such ancestors. One was my great-grandfather John Bennion. We cannot duplicate what he did because the world has changed, but we can learn from it.

He was a convert to the Church from Wales. He, his wife, and his children came into the Salt Lake Valley in one of the early companies of pioneers. We know something of his life because after that time he kept a journal, making a short entry nearly every day. We have the journals from 1855 to 1877. They were published in one bound volume because his descendants hoped to transmit that legacy of testimony. My mother was one of them. Her last labor before she died was to transform the day books in which he'd written into a manuscript for publication.

His short entries don't have much preaching in them. He doesn't testify that he knew Brigham Young was a prophet. He just records having answered "yes" every time the prophet called him on a mission from "over Jordan" to the Muddy mission, then on to a mission back to Wales. He also answered "yes" to the call to ride into the canyons to track Johnston's army and the call to take his family south when the army invaded the valley. There is even a family legend that the reason he died so close to the day when Brigham Young was buried was to follow the prophet one more time.

The fact that he wrote every day makes clear to me that he knew his ordinary life was historic because it was part of the building of Zion in the latter days. The few entries which record his testimony seem to appear when death took a child. His testimony is to me more powerful because he offered it when his soul was tried.

Here is his record of one of those times. His daughter Elizabeth died in his arms. He reported her burial and the location of her grave in a few lines. But then, the next day, November 4, 1863, this is the entire entry: "Wednesday. Repairing up the stable my little children pratling around me but I miss my dear Lizzy. I pray the Lord to help me to indure faithfull to his cause to the end of my days, that I may be worthy to receive my children back into the family circle, who have fallen asleep in Christ in the days of their innocence Ann, Moroni, Esther Ellen & Elizabeth, blessed & happy are they because of the atonement of Jesus Christ."

All the elements are there. He taught the truth. He testified that it was true. He lived consistent with his testimony, and prayed that he might endure faithful until he could be united with his dear family. I feel his love and a desire to be included in that circle.

We must find other ways to convey our legacy of testimony, but the process of teaching, testifying, and living the truth will be the same. The scriptures, living prophets, and common sense tell us where to begin. We need to start with

177

ourselves as parents. No program we follow or family tradition we create can transmit a legacy of testimony we do not have. We must start where Alma started, so that our descendants can know that we testified from the same ground from which he testified. Here are his words as recorded in the Book of Mormon. It is what we must be able to say: "And this is not all. Do ye not suppose that I know of these things myself? Behold, I testify unto you that I do know that these things whereof I have spoken are true. And how do ye suppose that I know of their surety? Behold, I say unto you they are made known unto me by the Holy Spirit of God. Behold, I have fasted and prayed many days that I might know these things of myself. And now I do know of myself that they are true; for the Lord God hath made them manifest unto me by his Holy Spirit; and this is the spirit of revelation which is in me." (Alma 5:45–46.)

As we gain that assurance, most settings we will be in with our families will be good ones to create a legacy of testimony. Some of the best are already familiar to us. Here are some ways to make those common settings more likely to invite the experiences which bring testimony to our families.

First, plan for our weekly family night to be a setting for the bearing of testimony. Be sure that some truth of the gospel of Jesus Christ is taught simply and plainly, so that even a child could understand. A child could do the teaching. The child may choose to end with a testimony, if that is the way we end our teaching. A shy child may not easily bear testimony in larger settings but may in the safety of our homes. And the Holy Ghost will testify to those who hear and to the child who testifies.

Second, read the scriptures aloud together as a family. It may take unusual determination and inspiration to find a time and a setting. But reading and hearing the words of life from the scriptures will invite the Holy Ghost to confirm their truth. The Savior said it this way: "Search the scriptures; for in them ye think ye have eternal life: and they are they which testify of me." (John 5:39.)

Years ago, President Marion G. Romney recounted reading the Book of Mormon aloud, alternating paragraphs with his young son, he on the bottom level of a double-decker bed and his son on the upper. He thought his son was catching a cold, but then he learned that the tears came from his son feeling testimony that the book was true. And because they read together, both were blessed. (See *Conference Report*, April 1949, p. 41.)

Third, kneel together in humble prayer as a family, each having the opportunity to be voice. There may be times when the prayer seems rote and when those not praying let their minds wander. But there will be other priceless moments when someone will petition in faith for real needs and the Holy Ghost will touch hearts with testimony. I don't remember as much of my mother's teachings as I do her prayers for us. I could feel her love, and the Spirit confirmed in my heart that she loved Heavenly Father and the Savior and that her prayers would be answered. She brought blessings down on our heads then, and the memory of her prayers still does.

Fourth, fast and allow your children to fast once a month before the meeting in which they will partake of the Lord's Supper, hear others bear testimony, and perhaps themselves feel prompted to testify. The spiritual blessing will be even greater for them if they know that their choice to overcome their physical desires for food is making possible the caring for the poor. That can't happen unless we pay a generous fast offering with a joyful heart. It can if we do. And the likelihood will be greatly increased that they will feel the Spirit confirm that this is the true Church of

Jesus Christ if we have first taught and testified that the Savior always organized his disciples to care for the poor and the needy among them.

We could extend the list of things to do to invite the confirmation of the Holy Spirit. For instance, the warmth and confidence with which we receive home teachers can allow our children to feel confirmation that they come as God's servants. The giving of priesthood blessings as children start a school year or leave home invites the Spirit at a time when hearts are humble and thus receptive to the whisperings of the Spirit.

Some of the greatest opportunities to create and transmit a legacy of testimony cannot be planned. Tragedy, loss, and hurt often arrive unanticipated. How we react when we are surprised will tell our families whether what we have taught and testified lies deep in our hearts. Most of us will have taught our children of the power of the Savior to carry us through whatever befalls us. These words are from the Book of Mormon: "And he will take upon him death, that he may loose the bands of death which bind his people; and he will take upon him their infirmities, that his bowels may be filled with mercy, according to the flesh, that he may know according to the flesh how to succor his people according to their infirmities." (Alma 7:12.)

When tragedy strikes or even when it looms, our families will have the opportunity to look into our hearts to see whether we know what we said we knew. Our children will watch, feel the Spirit confirm that we lived as we preached, remember that confirmation, and pass the story across the generations.

I have one such story in my legacy. Grandmother Eyring learned from a doctor in his office that she would die of stomach cancer. My father, her oldest son, had driven her there and was waiting for her. He told me that on the way home she said, "Now, Henry, let's be cheerful. Let's sing hymns." They sang "O My Father" and "Come, Come, Ye Saints," where the last verse begins, "And should we die before our journey's through . . ."

I wasn't there, but I imagine they sang loudly—they didn't have very melodic voices—with faith and no tears. She spent part of her last months in the home of her oldest child, her daughter. Aunt Camilla told me that Grandma complained only once, and then it was not really a complaint, but just to say that it hurt.

Now, there are many people who have been cheerful and brave in the face of death. But it means far more to a family when the person has taught and testified of the power of the Savior to succor, of the sureness of the Resurrection, and of the hope of eternal life. The Spirit confirmed to me that Grandma's peace and her courage were signs that her testimony was true, and because of that, all was well, all was well.

Sadly, each of us knows that even teaching, testifying, and living true to that testimony may not pass on the legacy. Great and good parents have done that and then seen their families or some in their families reject that testimony. There is reason for us to have great hope and optimism. It comes first from our testimony of the nature of our Heavenly Father: he loves our family members; he is their Heavenly Father as well as ours. It also comes from our testimony of the mission of Jesus Christ: he paid the price to redeem them. And it comes from our testimony of the restoration of priesthood keys. Because of that, the power is on the earth again to make covenants with God that seal families together, covenants which God honors.

That is why we must not despair. As we offer the legacy of testimony to our families, some may not receive it. It may even seem to skip over generations. But God will reach out

181

to offer the legacy again and again. More than we can imagine, our faithful effort to offer to our family the testimony we have of the truth will be multiplied in power and extended in time.

We have all seen evidence of that in families we have known. I saw it in South America as I looked into the faces of missionaries. Hundreds of them passed by me, shaking my hand and looking deeply into my eyes. I was nearly overwhelmed with the confirmation that these children of Father Lehi and of Sariah were there in the Lord's service because our Heavenly Father honors his promises to families. To nearly his last breath, Lehi taught and testified and tried to bless his children. Terrible tragedy came among his descendants when they rejected his testimony and the testimonies of other prophets and of the scriptures. But in the eyes and faces of those missionaries I felt confirmation that God has kept his promises to reach out to Lehi's covenant children—and that he will reach out to ours.

I testify that God, our Heavenly Father, lives and that he loves us and know us. I know that Jesus Christ lives, and that we will be resurrected and can be sanctified because of his sacrifice. I testify that we can know the truth by the power of the Holy Ghost. I know that we can live together in families in eternal life, the greatest of all the gifts of God. I pray that we may, with all our hearts for all our lives, offer testimony of the truth to our families.

CHAPTER 15

TO TOUCH A LIFE
WITH FAITH

In the April 1995 general conference, President Gordon B. Hinckley said: "This church does not belong to its President. Its head is the Lord Jesus Christ, whose name each of us has taken upon ourselves. We are all in this great endeavor together. We are here to assist our Father in His work and His glory, 'to bring to pass the immortality and eternal life of man' (Moses 1:39). Your obligation is as serious in your sphere of responsibility as is my obligation in my sphere. No calling in this church is small or of little consequence. All of us in the pursuit of our duty touch the lives of others. To each of us in our respective responsibilities the Lord has said: 'Wherefore, be faithful; stand in the office which I have appointed unto you; succor the weak, lift up the hands which hang down, and strengthen the feeble knees' (D&C 81:5)." (*Conference Report,* April 1995, p. 94; or *Ensign,* May 1995, p. 71.)

You must have wondered about that idea that your calling carries for you as serious a responsibility as his does for

---

From a talk given at General Conference, 30 September 1995.

him. But you can see why that must be so. You and he are
called by the same Savior, whose church this is. You are
involved in the same work, which is to help the Lord to
bring to pass the eternal life of man. In your calling you
touch lives. The life you touch in your service will be as
valuable to God as any other life. And so how you touch a
life is as serious a matter for you as it would be for any other
servant of God.

That seriousness comes from your assigned purpose.
Your responsibility is to touch people so that they will make
the choices that will take them toward eternal life. And
eternal life is the greatest of all the gifts of God.

You may feel uncomfortable with the thought that what
may seem to you simple assignments or everyday acts could
have eternal consequences. But you may have done more
than you know. During a stake conference I attended, a
man came up to me and described in detail how someone
had once helped his grandson return to activity in the
Church. A young deacon had been asked by his quorum
president to bring to a Sunday meeting a boy who had
never attended. The deacon trudged up to the boy's house,
got him to come to church a few times, and then saw him
move away. He may have thought he hadn't done much
that mattered. But more than ten years later and almost a
continent away, the boy's grandfather asked me, with tears
in his eyes, if I could give his thanks to that deacon, now
grown older, unaware that the Savior had reached out
through a twelve-year-old servant assigned by a thirteen-
year-old quorum president.

You may know the feelings of that grandfather. The
mother of his grandson was raising him alone with no contact with the Church. That grandfather had tried every way
he knew to reach out to touch their lives. He loved them.
He felt responsibility for them. And he knew what you

know: he knew that someday, when they saw things as they really are, they would wish with all their hearts that they had made the choices that would qualify them for eternal life, choices which won't and can't be made without faith in Jesus Christ sufficient to salvation.

His heartache was one most of us have felt over someone we cared about and could not seem to reach. And that heartache will lead you to ponder and pray for the answer to this question: How can I touch a life with faith?

A place to begin your pondering is with the Savior and his disciples. Early in his mortal ministry, they wanted him to touch their lives with faith. "And the apostles said unto the Lord, Increase our faith. And the Lord said, If ye had faith as a grain of mustard seed, ye might say unto his sycamine tree, Be thou plucked up by the root, and be thou planted in the sea; and it should obey you." (Luke 17:5–6.)

You will not be surprised that the Lord responded by speaking of a seed. The first thing to know about how faith in him increases is to think of its growth like that of a tree. You remember how Alma used that illustration. The seed is the word of God. It must be planted in the heart of the person you serve and whose faith you want to see increase. He described what must happen this way: "Now, we will compare the word unto a seed. Now, if ye give place, that a seed may be planted in your heart, behold, if it be a true seed, or a good seed, if ye do not cast it out by your unbelief, that ye will resist the Spirit of the Lord, behold, it will begin to swell within your breasts; and when you feel these swelling motions, ye will begin to say within yourselves—It must needs be that this is a good seed, or that the word is good, for it beginneth to enlarge my soul; yea, it beginneth to enlighten my understanding, yea, it beginneth to be delicious to me. Now behold, would not this increase your faith? I say unto you, Yea." (Alma 32:28–29.)

Just as soil needs preparation for a seed, so does a human heart for the word of God to take root. Before he told the people to plant the seed, Alma told them that their hearts were prepared. They had been persecuted and cast out of their churches. Alma with his love and the circumstances of their lives, which led them to be humble, had prepared them. They were then ready to hear the word of God. If they chose to plant it in their hearts, the growth in their souls would surely follow, and that would increase their faith.

It's not hard to see from these examples what you can do to touch someone's life with faith. To begin with, you recognize that what people choose to do, and what the Savior has done, will matter more than what you do. But there are things you can do to make it more likely that they will make the choices that will move them toward eternal life.

You know first of all that to plant the seed, they must do more than hear the word of God. They have to try it by keeping the commandments. The Lord said it this way: "Jesus answered them, and said, My doctrine is not mine, but his that sent me. If any man will do his will, he shall know of the doctrine, whether it be of God, or whether I speak of myself." (John 7:16–17.)

It won't be enough for them simply to listen to the word of God. They must choose to keep commandments because they feel at least a beginning desire to know the will of our Heavenly Father and submit to it. That feeling of surrender is not likely to come unless they experience some feeling of being loved and some value in their being meek and lowly of heart.

You can help with your example. If you love them because you feel God's love for them, they will feel that. If

186

you are meek and humble because you feel your dependence on God, they will sense that, too.

In addition to your example, you can teach the word of God to them in a way that is more likely to give them a desire to repent and to try to live it. They may think they have heard preaching enough. But they must do more than hear the word of God; they must plant it in their hearts by trying it. You can make that more likely if you talk with them about it in a way that helps them feel how much God loves them and how much they need God.

Aaron, one of the great missionaries in the Book of Mormon, knew how to teach that way. You remember how he taught King Lamoni's father, the old king. The king's heart had already been prepared by seeing love and humility in the way Aaron's brother had treated Lamoni, his son. But even with that preparation of the old king's heart, Aaron taught the word of God in a way to emphasize God's love and our need for him: "And it came to pass that when Aaron saw that the king would believe his words, he began from the creation of Adam, reading the scriptures unto the king—how God created man after his own image, and that God gave him commandments, and that because of transgression, man had fallen. And Aaron did expound unto him the scriptures from the creation of Adam, laying the fall of man before him, and their carnal state and also the plan of redemption, which was prepared from the foundation of the world, through Christ, for all whosoever would believe on his name." (Alma 22:12–13.)

You won't very often have the remarkable result that Aaron had. After hearing the word of God taught that way, in what the scriptures sometimes call the plan of happiness, the old king said that he would give whatever he had to root the wickedness out of him and have eternal life. When Aaron told him to cry to God in prayer for forgiveness, the king bowed down on the spot. The seed was planted. He was doing the will of God. (See verses 15–18.)

When you touch the hearts of people you serve, you won't do everything exactly the way Aaron did. But you will do some of the same things. You will try to help them feel that God loves them by the way you treat them. You will be humble so that they are more likely to choose to be meek and lowly of heart. You will teach the word of God, when the Spirit prompts you, in a way that testifies of God's love for them and their need for the atonement of Jesus Christ. And you will teach them commandments they can keep. That is why, when you go into the mission field, you learn to commit those you teach to pray or to read the Book of Mormon or to come with you to a sacrament meeting or to be baptized. You know that when they keep commandments they plant the seed. And you know that it will grow, their souls will be expanded, and when that happens their faith will increase.

You not only know what to do, but you know when the Spirit is apt to prompt you to do it. The times people will be most likely to choose to try the word of God, to repent, will be when they feel at least the beginnings of his love for them and their dependence on him.

For instance, wise bishops have learned that funerals can be such times. When death occurs in a family, the bishop, quorum members, and the home teachers and visiting teachers reach out to the family because they love them. The family generally feel humbled, longing for comfort and peace. For many, their hearts will be prepared to hear the word of God.

The bishop will know that as he plans the funeral service. He will be sure that testimony is given of the plan of salvation, of the atonement of Jesus Christ, of the Resurrection, and of glorious reunions, because that will bring comfort and hope. But such teaching will do more than that. The word of God will be heard by people with hearts softened by love and by grief and so more likely to choose living it more fully. And from their doing that, faith will increase and the changes will come which move them toward eternal life.

Your opportunities won't come only at times of great tragedy or overwhelming need. Life has in it moments of challenge that will bring even the people most hardened to spiritual things to say to themselves, "Isn't there more than this?" If you have been a constant friend, if you have proved your love by service and so become trusted, they may turn to you with that question. When they do, you can say, knowing that their hearts are prepared, "Yes, there is, and I can tell you where it is and what you can do to find it."

Your teaching will become easier as those you serve try the word of God. For instance, a deacon or an elder might choose to follow the command to search the scriptures and so read passages that tell him of the honor and glory bestowed through the holy priesthood. (See D&C 124:34.) From such obedience in reading scriptures, he might be able to hear the Holy Ghost whisper that such an honor, such a holy calling, deserves wearing better than everyday clothes when he performs priesthood ordinances or more considerate speech wherever he is. Because others may not honor the dignity of the priesthood in those ways, such obedience may take faith. But faith when exercised increases. And that increase in faith will give greater power to hear and to obey.

Now, you will have great moments in your service to others as they discover the source of faith or when that faith leads them to go through the pain of repentance to gain the peace of forgiveness. But even people with faith developed by obedience and with sins washed away will

189

need your help to refresh and strengthen their faith. There are reasons for that. Blessings, when they are no longer seen as coming from our Heavenly Father, can lead to pride. The peace of forgiveness can lead to overconfidence and to forgetting to pray always lest we be overcome. Even some who have exercised faith enough to have great spiritual experiences have later been deceived into apostasy or overcome by the trials of life. All of them need your help in nurturing faith, in learning to put all their trust in God.

For all those you serve, wherever they may be in the tests of life, the way you nurture will be much the same. You will love them. You will encourage them as they choose to be humble. You will present the word of God to them in the way most likely to lead to their choosing to exercise enough faith to repent and thus see that there is more that God would have them do. And that will help them endure in faith.

Now, your responsibility to touch lives might seem overwhelming. You can take heart that you were called by the Savior. You have the same promise he gave those he called at the beginning of his earthly ministry. He called first humble men, uneducated, with less schooling and less gospel knowledge than the most recently ordained of you may have. But consider what he said, and know that it applies to you: "And Jesus, walking by the sea of Galilee, saw two brethren, Simon called Peter, and Andrew his brother, casting a net into the sea: for they were fishers. And he saith unto them, Follow me, and I will make you fishers of men. And they straightway left their nets, and followed him." (Matthew 4:18–20.)

He will make you a fisher of men, however inadequate you may feel now. It won't be done by a mysterious process. It will be the natural result of your choosing to follow him. Just think about what you must do to be a fisher of men, to touch lives with faith for him. You will need to love the people you serve. You will need to be humble and full of hope. You will need to have the Holy Ghost as your companion to know when to speak and what to say and how to testify.

But all of that will come naturally, in time, from the covenants you make and keep as you follow him. (See Moroni 8:25–26.) And in the process you will experience a mighty change of heart. You may not have seen that mighty change in yourself yet. But it will come as you continue to follow him. You can trust that he will qualify you as his servant, to assist him in touching lives with faith to bring to pass the eternal life of man. And you will find satisfaction in that service beyond your fondest dreams.

INDEX

Aaron, 187–88
Afflictions, 76, 180–81
Agency, 52–53, 133
Alma, 130, 149–50
Arrogance, 85–86
Atonement: making, work in life, 46–50, 53–59, 108–9, 132–33, 170–71; effects of, 51–52, 155; and change of heart, 70–71; expressing gratitude for, 79–80; bearing testimony of, 149–50

Baptism, 49, 118
Bauer, Ray, 61–62
Benjamin, King, 76–77
Bennion, John, 6–7, 176–77
Benson, Ezra Taft, 70–71
Blessings: counting, as way of remembrance, 78–79; trials as, 84–85; patriarchal, example of, 135–36; from priesthood, 180
Book of Mormon, 38, 118, 147–48. See also Alma, Mormon, Nephi
Book of Remembrance. See Journals

Callings, Church: not being overwhelmed by, 3–5; accepting others', 9–10; learning from others', 11–13; helping others in, 14–21; fulfilling, to receive Holy Ghost, 50, 58–59; importance of, 183–85. See also Servants, mortal
Celestial kingdom, 162
Central America branch, 29–30
Certainties in life, 82–83, 87–88
Chance, 81
Change of heart: discerning, 53–59; in repenting, 64–65; through the Atonement, 70–71; in drawing on powers of heaven, 95–96; as surrendering to Christ, 105–7
Charity, 71, 80
Chastisement, 51, 85–86
Children, 163–64
Choices, 34–35, 98–103, 133, 136–37, 153
Clark, J. Reuben, 143–45
Cleanliness, 64, 115
Commandments. See Obedience
Confession, 49, 136–37